Praise for *Predicting Jesus*

If you're longing to grow an intimate relationship with a trustworthy God during uncertain times, choose *Predicting Jesus* as your next Bible study. Kim Erickson skillfully makes prophecy understandable and points us to a God who does not break His promises. The book of Isaiah will capture your heart and bring peace to your soul as you're reminded that when times are tough, God is still in control. This book is excellent for self-study, but even better when shared with a group of friends in a small group study. Don't miss it!

CAROL KENT | Founder of Speak Up Conference, speaker, and author, *Becoming a Woman of Influence*

How do I learn to trust someone? When they keep their word and come through on their promises. Kim has provided a sturdy and solid framework for us to witness firsthand the trustworthiness of God in fulfilling His promises through Christ Jesus. This study will embolden your faith, build your trust in God's timing, and invite you to rest securely in His unshakable love for you. If you are ready for fresh wonder over the beauty of Christ, don't miss this study!

ERICA WIGGENHORN | National Speaker and author of *An Unexpected Revival*, an eight-week study through the prophecies of Ezekiel

Kim has written another enlightening book that draws you into personal joy and wonder at the cross, and the majesty of God's healing and redeeming power through Jesus. I found this study of Isaiah both scholarly and personal, linking the prophecies with the New Testament fulfillments while enriching your faith as it has for Kim and millions of others. Uniquely, *Predicting Jesus* is a personal journey through Isaiah, taking you deeper into the most meaningful adventure of all—life and relationship with Jesus. Read. Discuss. Enjoy!

CHUCK PETERMAN | Lead Minister of Creekside Christian Church, Jacksonville, FL

One thing people often miss about the Bible, especially the first thirty-nine books of it, is that the entire Bible speaks of Jesus. Kim Erickson, in her wonderful new Bible study, *Predicting Jesus*, looks at the book of Isaiah and its many prophecies of the coming Messiah and walks you through the power of His words today. It will encourage you, strengthen you in your faith, and give you understanding and clarity to all that Jesus accomplished for you in His life and death. She will also remind you of the prophecies yet to be fulfilled when Jesus returns and sets up His kingdom, that day that you and I are to live for in this life. I highly commend this study to you.

STEVE ENGRAM | Senior Pastor, Desert Springs Community Church, Goodyear, AZ

Kim Erickson once again demonstrates her deep love for the Lord and understanding of the Word. In *Predicting Jesus*, she unpacks the "Jesus prophecies" in Isaiah in terms that even a new believer can understand. She relies not only on her personal study of the Bible and lets Scripture interpret Scripture, but she also shares with her readers what reliable scholars and commentators have written about some of the more difficult passages. I found this study of the messianic prophecies of Isaiah informative, enjoyable, and life changing.

KATHLEEN DUNCAN | Coauthor of *God's Healing in Grief* and author of *Fun Brain Games for Adults*

God is a Promise-Keeper you can trust. Bravo to Kim Erickson for pointing me to Isaiah's prophecies about Jesus fulfilled (and to her own personal faith journey) that prove it! Kim's six-week Bible study, *Predicting Jesus*, will encourage and equip you with biblical truth needed now more than ever to stand firm in our world of uncertainty. It will also enlarge your faith and challenge you to apply what you learn and trust God more—until Jesus returns. This interactive study is perfect for anyone—from skeptic to seasoned Christ follower.

KATHE WUNNENBERG | President/Founder, Hopelifters Unlimited

The *Predicting Jesus* Bible study offers insight into the prophecies of God through Isaiah. Kim shares the comforting reminder that the act of prophecy is more than just God sharing and preparing us for what will happen. Prophecy is also our lifeline of hope in God as these things come to pass. During turbulent seasons, when the weight of this broken world feels heavy, this reminder feels like a big hug from our father as we journey through life. I am grateful for a loving God and for the ways He is using Kim to help us dig deeper into His Word.

RACHEL BRAGG | Mentor to women and couples with her husband, and leader of Bible study groups

For a Bible study leader, *Predicting Jesus* gives a biblical, discerning, and practical resource for Bible study. It is sure to generate thoughtful discussion, specific life application, and great hope for members of your group. Kim Erickson's writing style provides an easy read while incorporating solid hermeneutics—engaging for every level of Bible study participant.

LINDA PERSANDI | Christian counselor and Bible study leader

I have known Kim Erickson from the beginning of her faith journey with Jesus and deeply respect her quest to know God through His Word. In *Predicting Jesus*, you will find the messianic prophecies of Isaiah to be thought-provoking, enlightening, and life changing. You will be enriched in your love of Jesus and trust in God as you delve into this study from the book of Isaiah. Highly recommend it for personal or group studies.

SHARON ENGRAM | Bible teacher, speaker, and coauthor, *Surviving Widowhood: 40 Devotions of Hope*

PREDICTING JESUS

A 6-Week Study of the Messianic Prophecies of Isaiah

Kim Erickson

MOODY PUBLISHERS
CHICAGO

Edited by Pamela Joy Pugh
Interior design: Kaylee Dunn
Cover design: Charles Brock and Erik M. Peterson
Cover and interior image of scroll copyright © 2022 by Anna Sedneva/Shutterstock (71999587). All rights reserved.
Author photo: Daisy Moffat Photography

Library of Congress Cataloging-in-Publication Data

Names: Erickson, Kim, 1970- author.
Title: Predicting Jesus : a 6-week study of the Messianic prophecies of
    Isaiah / Kim Erickson.
Description: Chicago : Moody Publishers, [2022] | Includes bibliographical
    references. | Summary: "Predicting Jesus is a six-week women's Bible
    study from author and Bible teacher Kim Erickson on the book of Isaiah.
    It is a verse-by-verse study of Isaiah's prophecies about Jesus and
    their fulfillment in the New Testament. It also includes contemporary
    application, weekly homework, reflection and prayer, and discussion
    questions for possible weekly small group interaction. Teaching on
    Isaiah is deeply personal to Kim as reading through it was
    transformative in the aftermath of her young son's death: "Reading so
    many words that actually came true, some hundreds of years later,
    confirmed the character of God for me. Deep in my heart, I finally let
    go. I let go of the world's effort to shame me into thinking it was all
    a sham. I let go of human logic. I let go of the paralysis of analysis.
    The focus of this study-Isaiah's prophecies regarding Christ-reveal so
    much about God: His power, His nature, His plans. We can trust Him to do
    what He says He is going to do. I pray women use this book to challenge
    their current mindsets, check their understanding, and push forward in
    their faith in Jesus and the Bible.""-- Provided by publisher.
Identifiers: LCCN 2022002442 (print) | LCCN 2022002443 (ebook) | ISBN
    9780802425119 | ISBN 9780802476586 (ebook)
Subjects: LCSH: Bible. Isaiah--Prophecies--Textbooks. |
    Messiah--Prophecies--Biblical teaching--Textbooks. | Bible.
    Isaiah--Relation to the New Testament--Textbooks. | Bible. New
    Testament--Relation to Isaiah--Textbooks. | BISAC: RELIGION / Biblical
    Studies / Prophecy | RELIGION / Christian Living / Spiritual Growth
Classification: LCC BS1515.6.M44 E75 2022 (print) | LCC BS1515.6.M44
    (ebook) | DDC 224/.106--dc23/eng/20220322
LC record available at https://lccn.loc.gov/2022002442
LC ebook record available at https://lccn.loc.gov/2022002443

Originally delivered by fleets of horse-drawn wagons, the affordable paperbacks from D. L. Moody's publishing house resourced the church and served everyday people. Now, after more than 125 years of publishing and ministry, Moody Publishers' mission remains the same—even if our delivery systems have changed a bit. For more information on other books (and resources) created from a biblical perspective, go to www.moodypublishers.com or write to:

Moody Publishers
820 N. LaSalle Boulevard
Chicago, IL 60610

1 3 5 7 9 10 8 6 4 2

Printed in the United States of America

In loving memory of Pastor Don Engram, who helped settle the issue of "Thus sayeth the Lord" in my heart through his passionate preaching and love for the Lord.

This study is dedicated to Devin, my husband and partner in every way. Thank you for your unflinching support when I take on hard things! You never hesitate to get behind my ideas. You never question God's call on my life to study, write, and teach. I couldn't do any of this without you. Much love from across the room!

CONTENTS

GETTING STARTED:

Why Study the Prophecies in Isaiah?   8

Brief Overview of the Book of Isaiah   12

How Jesus Used the Prophecies   14

WEEK ONE: The Savior Is Coming   18

WEEK TWO: The Savior Will Conquer Sin and Death   50

WEEK THREE: The Savior with Us   80

WEEK FOUR: The Savior's Strength and Love   113

WEEK FIVE: The Savior's Sacrifice   144

WEEK SIX: The Savior's Everlasting Peace   173

CLOSING EXERCISE   198

CLOSING COMMENTS   199

WITH GREAT GRATITUDE   200

NOTES   202

Why Study the Prophecies in Isaiah?

Prophecy. Not the easiest word or concept, no matter if you're a seasoned reader of Scripture, just getting started, or frankly skeptical. But prophecy is a key tool used by God to help us with our unbelief. Let me explain.

Using prophecy to dispel unbelief worked for me in my faith journey, which began just after losing our three-year-old son, Austin, to complications with strep throat. It's fair to say that the book of Isaiah became the rock of my faith in Jesus and the Bible as God's Word. My lawyer mind demanded *proof* that God was real, and that Jesus was my Savior. As a grieving mom, I needed assurance that God *will* come through on His promises. Without God's promises, without the certainty of heaven, life without Austin would be too much to bear—too long and too painful without the assurance of an eternal life where there is no more death, no more mourning, and no more pain. My mental health as a grieving mom depends on the expectation of that future. Any joy or peace I can grasp in this life is grounded in prophecy already fulfilled by Jesus and prophecy yet to be fulfilled when He comes back—and He *is* coming back!

The book of Isaiah is where my new-believer mind and grieving-mom heart grasped onto the hope offered by God. The book of Isaiah details the whole human story and reveals the magnificence of our loving God's plan all in one place. I can't wait to show you how!

Studying the ancient words of Isaiah removed the remaining skepticism from my heart when I was a new believer in Christ. Reading so many words that actually came true—hundreds of years after they were written—confirmed the character of God for me. Deep in my heart, I finally let go. I let go of the world's effort to bluff me into thinking it was all a sham. Let go of human logic. Let go of the paralysis of analysis. Let go of striving to understand everything in my mind.

What about you? Where would you put yourself on this scale regarding prophecies in general?

- ☐ Open to exploring prophecies and considering what they might mean, but still a bit unsure if they're even true or matter to my faith

- ☐ Frankly somewhat or very skeptical; could prophecies really have been written hundreds of years before predicted events came about?

- ☐ Already believe in God's Word and am interested in learning more, even about hard things

- ☐ Other

Consider sharing your responses during your first small group meeting. It's a good idea to get a feel for who in your group has more experience with Scripture and/or belief in prophecy and who is more skeptical. I think it's okay to question and ponder as you study the Bible. It's okay if you're skeptical and struggling to believe. It's better that you wrestle with the material than disregard it altogether. Deep, difficult discussions in a safe place (as women's Bible studies should be) only serve to strengthen your faith and the faith of those around you. There is no judgment here! Only a desire to know God more intimately is required for this study.

So why are we studying Isaiah? Through the prophet Isaiah, God has already promised us a future and a glorious hope. My prayer is that studying these prophecies in Isaiah will set your trust in God, like cement for your soul, never shaken.

My hope for your heart is that studying Isaiah settles the matter of surrender for you, that any pieces of yourself you've held back from God will finally (and joyfully) be placed into the hands that created the heavens and the earth. He alone is trustworthy with *all* of your heart and your hopes. You can be bold, more confident in your proclamation that Jesus is our Savior.

Isaiah's words make me awestruck by a God who was rejected, and mocked time and time again, and yet would humble Himself to save us from our own self-centeredness. A God who would never, *ever* break His covenant. A God who yearns to be at the center of our lives. A God who will restore humankind, not because we deserve it, but because He said He would. Complete healing and eternal glory await the believer by the sheer fact of His Word. Heaven awaits because God said so.

Just because He said so. *This* is why I study the book of Isaiah the most when my heart is hurting. I want to come alongside you and offer a look at the God we serve through the words of the prophet Isaiah. You will love the book of Isaiah.

Studying the book of Isaiah reminds us that *only God* can predict the future, determine the fate of nations, and hold humankind accountable. Only God deserves our complete trust and surrender.

Isaiah spoke of difficult times for the Jewish people and their nation, but he also spoke of a mighty Creator-Redeemer who cares for His people with lovingkindness. God spoke through Isaiah so that the Jewish people would trust God when the tough times came, knowing that their God would never forsake His promises to bring restoration to His people. Holding on to this truth was vital when the nation would be taken into captivity in Babylon, as we'll read about in the overview below. Isaiah was speaking *before* this event.

I love how John Oswalt put it:

> [The Jewish] people needed to hear the Word of God in ways that
> changed how they thought. That is what we need too. We need lives
> of faith that are shaped by the Word of God, its view of reality, and

the principles that emerge from it. If I cannot "believe" God and "hope" in him in the sense of surrendering my life to him in a kind of life that I know pleases him, then his power cannot transform me. But if I will actively believe in his Word, there really are no limits to what he can do for me, for my family, and for my society.[1]

The focus of this study—Isaiah's prophecies regarding Christ—reveals so much about God, His power, His nature, and His plans. As He shows Himself to us, we begin to understand that God is the only true God. He alone is worthy and able. We can trust Him to do what He says He is going to do. And our Creator-Redeemer is coming back.

Perhaps as much as the Jewish people exiled in Babylon, Christians in today's world need to be reminded that our mighty God is trustworthy, that He *always* does what He says He's going to do. Victory is certain. Studying these prophecies will help you gain a deeper understanding of the mighty God we serve. Studying the Scriptures that foretold the Messiah removed the skepticism from my mind and heart. The fulfilled prophecies regarding Christ (and many other historical and verifiable events) convinced me that the Bible is true, holy, and God-breathed. No one else but God could get that many things right about Jesus, His life, and His death so many years even before His birth. The Bible very simply became the Word of God to me *because* of the fulfilled prophecies about Jesus.

How about you? Do you think there is proof that Jesus was who He claimed to be, the Son of God? Do you waver a bit when it comes to putting your confidence in the Bible? Perhaps you're a strong believer and you want to go deeper into the messianic prophecies in the Old Testament. Or maybe you want to grow in your knowledge and understanding of how the Old and New Testaments go together. Do you want to expand your faith? Do you want to become bolder for Christ? Or perhaps you're just not sure about any of this and you came to learn!

Use this Bible study to challenge your current mindset, check your understanding, and push you forward in your faith in Jesus and the Bible.

Brief Overview
of the Book of Isaiah

THE PROPHET

The name "Isaiah" means "Jehovah saves" or "Salvation of Jehovah." It is believed that Isaiah was from a prominent family, or perhaps even related to the royal family of Judah, because of his apparent influence among the rulers of Judah. Isaiah is sometimes called the "prince of prophets" for this reason. He was married ("prophetess" is referenced in Isa. 8:3) and had two sons (7:3 and 8:3).

Isaiah is considered a "major" prophet of the Bible (along with Jeremiah, Ezekiel, and Daniel) as opposed to the "minor" prophets (Obadiah, Joel, Jonah, Amos, Hosea, Micah, Nahum, Zephaniah, Habakkuk, Haggai, Zechariah, and Malachi). These prophets are not divided based on significance of the messages, however, but rather simply by the length of their books.

Scholars also label prophets by the time period of their ministry as pre-exile, exile, or post-exile. Isaiah is considered a pre-exile prophet because he spoke the words contained in the sixty-six chapters of the book of Isaiah prior to the Jewish exile to Babylon. Isaiah made the most prophecies regarding the Jewish people and Christ. And he is the prophet who is most often quoted in the New Testament.

AUTHORSHIP AND STRUCTURE

Some scholars debate whether or not one man, Isaiah son of Amoz, actually wrote all sixty-six chapters of this book. Some say there must have been two or more authors due to the specific predictions that were fulfilled over time. These scholars insist multiple authors must have added to the scrolls to account for the fulfillment of the words in the book of Isaiah; in other words, someone snuck in and added prophecies after foretold events had already occurred. However, if you believe in the Holy Spirit and in God's ability to speak to and through His prophets, you can set aside this reasoning.

The book of Isaiah is divided into two major parts: judgment and restoration. In chapters 1–39, Isaiah speaks of the sins of the Jewish people and the consequences that will take place as a result. In chapters 40–66, Isaiah speaks God's message of comfort, hope, and restoration. God reminds His people that He is a faithful God who will keep His covenant with them.

Some point to the shift in tone and language used between chapters 1–39 and 40–66 as evidence of a different writer. But this can simply be attributed to the change in focus of the message. Isaiah shifts from the judgment of Judah in chapters 1–39 to God's comfort and restoration of the Jewish people in chapters 40–66. A change in tone and language beginning in chapter 40 makes sense to me because the message changed, and Isaiah was speaking to achieve a different purpose—to comfort and give hope.

THE TIME AND PLACE

Isaiah lived in the eighth century BC, during the time when Israel was a divided nation. After King Solomon's death, the ten northern tribes formed Israel, with its capital city being Samaria. The two remaining tribes of Benjamin and Judah united to become the southern kingdom, Judah, with Jerusalem as its capital.

Isaiah spoke mainly to Judah (but sometimes also to Israel) "in the days of Uzziah, Jotham, Ahaz, and Hezekiah, kings of Judah" (Isa.1:1). Thus, Isaiah's ministry as a prophet took place in the range of 740–680 BC,[2] during some very turbulent times for the Jewish people. There were threats to their safety and culture on all sides, including between and among the tribes themselves.

The northern kingdom of Israel was taken captive by Assyria in 721 BC. Then, the southern kingdom of Judah was defeated by Nebuchadnezzar, king of Babylon, in 586 BC. At this time, the capital, Jerusalem, major buildings, and the beautiful temple Solomon had built were all destroyed. Thousands of Jewish people were taken to Babylon for seventy years, a key event in the history of the Jewish people, known as the Babylonian captivity or exile.

Isaiah predicted these and other events long before they occurred. These and many other prophecies spoken by Isaiah[3] can be traced through secular, non-Christian sources. These fulfilled prophesies have a special place in my soul because they changed me from skeptic to sold out for Jesus. The words of Isaiah became undeniable proof to me that Jesus was the Messiah. By tracking the words in Isaiah through history and Jesus, I became confident that the Bible truly is the Word of God, written from the very breath of God Himself. My heart longs to pray over you as you read these words and wonder at our astonishing God.

How Jesus Used the Prophecies

"Do not think that I have come to abolish the Law or the Prophets;
I have not come to abolish them but to fulfill them." (Matt. 5:17)

Jesus pointed people to prophecies in the Old Testament to help them understand who He was and what was to come. An unforgettable scene that took place at the very beginning of His public ministry is recorded in Luke 4:16–21. At the synagogue, Jesus took the scroll and found Isaiah 61. He read the passage and made this astonishing declaration: *"Today this Scripture has been fulfilled in your hearing."*

Jesus was handed the scroll of Isaiah and unrolled it until He "found the place" (Luke 4:17) where the words summarized His mission, words that had been written more than six hundred years before He was born.

Jesus did something similar at the end of His time on earth, just following His resurrection: He turned to the prophecies in the Old Testament to explain Himself. Two disciples were walking on the way to Emmaus on the day of the resurrection and discussing everything that had happened to Jesus. A stranger met up with them (it was Jesus, but His identity was hidden from them until later) who asked what they were talking about. They described the recent events, astonished that someone in the region had not heard everything that had happened. Jesus said to them:

> "O foolish ones, and slow of heart to believe all that the prophets have spoken! Was it not necessary that the Christ should suffer these things and enter into his glory?" And beginning with Moses and all the Prophets, he interpreted to them in all the Scriptures the things concerning himself. (Luke 24:25–27)

In Old Testament times, God used prophecy to speak to His people, to make sure they would believe Him and trust Him. God *wants* us to understand Him and trust Him—and He uses prophecy to help us. In fact, in His final teaching in the upper room, Jesus referenced two Old Testament prophecies and *told* the disciples what was going to happen *so that* Scripture would be fulfilled. In John 13:18–19, just after washing the disciples' feet, Jesus told them:

> "But the Scripture will be fulfilled, 'He who ate my bread has lifted his heel against me.' I am telling you this now, before it takes place, that when it does take place you may believe that I am he."

"He who ate my bread has lifted his heel against me" was a prophecy from Psalm 41:9, which foretold, "Even my close friend in whom I trusted, who ate my bread, has lifted his heel against me." Jesus layered on the importance of prophecy by telling the disciples (three times during the Last Supper!) that He was telling them about His death and resurrection ahead of time so that when the events came to pass, they would believe that He is the Messiah.

A bit later that same night, Jesus told the disciples that the people had sinned because they hated Him, but then He added:

> "But the word that is written in their Law must be fulfilled:
> 'They hated me without a cause.'" (John 15:25)

Jesus is clear: prophecy *must* be fulfilled. In this same final teaching, Jesus makes a prophecy Himself: Peter will deny Him three times before the rooster crows. That's a very familiar passage, but have you ever thought about *why* Jesus made such a prediction? Perhaps it was another bit of evidence that He really was the Messiah. A prediction fulfilled is powerful evidence of the voice of God.

Let's turn to our Bibles and learn how Isaiah's words were predicting Jesus!

OPENING PRAYER

Lord, maker of heaven and earth, open my heart and my mind to the Scriptures. Let me see You, the only true God. Father, help me set aside my worldly reasoning and adopt childlike wonder at a God who loves me enough to tell me before things happen so that I may believe fully in Him alone. Capture my heart, O God. Rescue my soul, O Lord. I worship You, a great and mighty God. You alone are worthy. As I begin this study, I bow at Your throne, O God, and request that I may remain in Your presence while I ponder the prophecies of Christ. In the powerful name of Jesus I pray. Amen.

THE SAVIOR
IS COMING

We must begin our study with the promise of forgiveness because the whole point of Jesus coming to earth as a human was for the forgiveness of sins. The lifeblood of Jesus is the only atonement for sin that is acceptable to God. We'll really dive into this more during our lessons in Week Two, but we'll start with a prophecy in Isaiah 4 explaining the work of the Messiah. We'll start there because the need for atonement is the critical mission of the Messiah.

The chapters we will study this week (Isaiah 7–11) are sometimes referred to as "The Book of Immanuel." We will be studying the virgin birth (chapter 7), the divine King (chapter 9), and the perfect ruler and His glorious reign (chapter 11).[1]

One of the great debates about Jesus is whether He was just a man, a great teacher, a prophet, or the Messiah, the Savior for God's people. Many scoff and reject Jesus as the Messiah, the Son of God, because they reject the virgin birth of Jesus. "Impossible!" skeptics declare. "The girl, Mary, was lying, of course." Interestingly, even some Christian scholars have begun to disagree about the importance of this prophecy.

The logical among us also may argue that the other prophecies about the birthplace and genealogy of Jesus could have applied to many other babies at that time.

What many of those people fail to take into account, however, is that through the prophecies of Isaiah, God was telling the people of Judah how He was going to keep a promise He made to King David. As you study this week, keep this promise from God to David in mind:

> "When your days are fulfilled and you lie down with your fathers, I will raise up your offspring after you, who shall come from your body, and I will establish his kingdom. He shall build a house for my name, and I will establish the throne of his kingdom forever. I will be to him a father, and he shall be to me a son. When he commits iniquity, I will discipline him with the rod of men, with the stripes of the sons of men, but my steadfast love will not depart from him, as I took it from Saul, whom I put away from before you. And your house and your kingdom shall be made sure forever before me. Your throne shall be established forever." (2 Sam. 7:12–16)

Wait, is this prophecy about Jesus or Solomon? Both! The promise of a ruler who would be from the line of David, whose throne would last forever, was a well-known vision the prophet Nathan delivered to David. The building of the house of the Lord was a "near" prophecy that David's son, Solomon, would build the temple rather than David. You'll have to get used to this idea of both "near" and "far" prophecies mixed together because Isaiah does this a lot. I want you to explore for yourself exactly what Isaiah said about the Savior and discover why it matters to you in this modern day. Let's get started!

The Branch of the Lord

ISAIAH 4:2–6

Before you begin, ask God to give you eyes to see, ears to hear, and a heart to accept what He wants to teach you through the Scriptures today. Read the passage from Isaiah, looking for prophecies that could relate to the Messiah, His reign, or His kingdom. I recommend that you mark up your Bible as you do so. You might find it helpful to use colored pencils or highlighters to track themes or certain language. Take your time. Dig in!

READ ISAIAH 4:2–6.

"In that day" was a common phrase used by the prophets of Isaiah's time to signal a day coming in the future. That's really the only simple thing about this passage of Isaiah! There is so much to unpack, but we can do it. If you're using the English Standard Version, you'll notice that in verse 2, the "b" in branch is in lowercase. Interestingly, in the New American Standard and New International Version translations, the "b" in branch is capitalized so the phrase reads, "the Branch of the LORD."

With this subtle alteration, does it change how you see this passage and what (or whom) is being predicted? Why or why not?

Isaiah was the first to use this term, "the Branch of the LORD" (ṣemaḥ; YHWH), in the Old Testament.[2] The term was later used by Jeremiah (23:5; 33:15) and Zechariah (3:8; 6:12). Bible scholars, however, debate whether the term used, ṣemaḥ, really refers to the Messiah. But even some Jewish sages have given the term messianic meaning.[3] The literal word is, of course, "branch" as we understand it to be in terms of botany or regarding things that grow up from the ground. The primary argument that this phrase is *not* about the Messiah is because of the next phrase in that same sentence, "and fruit of the land." Those scholars who do not place messianic meaning on Isaiah 4:2–6 believe this passage related to the bountiful blessings that would flow upon Israel when the people repented and turned to God.[4]

One argument supporting that this phrase is about the Messiah, however, is that the Aramaic Targum translated this phrase as "Messiah of the Lord," "showing that the early Jewish interpreters thought this was a messianic reference."[5] (At some point Aramaic overshadowed Hebrew as the prominent language in the Jewish culture, so the Bible was translated from Hebrew to Aramaic for the "unlearned" Jews and was known as the Aramaic Targum.) Randall Price considered early traditions, later interpretations, the context and structure of Isaiah 4:2, along with other textual clues, and wrote that the connections "argue decisively for the messianic character of Isaiah 4:2."[6]

So, if you first read the above passage and didn't think it predicted anything about Jesus, you're not alone! Some scholars would agree with you. Yet, after studying several commentaries about this passage, I think Dr. Price and other commentators are correct in the opinion that this passage points to Jesus and the work of the Messiah.[7]

Assuming "the Branch of the LORD" *is* referring to Jesus, then what does the rest of this passage mean? Write your thoughts:

Stick with me here, because the glorious part for you and me is coming up! Not only does "washed away the filth of the daughters of Zion and cleansed the blood-stains of Jerusalem from its midst" mean the forgiveness of sins "by a spirit of judgment and by a spirit of burning" (the atoning sacrifice of Jesus on the cross), but these verses promise the protection of the Lord for all time, for all things. The passage is filled with beautiful imagery the Jewish people would have held near and dear.

In these verses, the Jewish people would have recognized Isaiah's references to the Shekinah glory of God that led them by cloud during the day and by fire at night during their wanderings in the desert. Also, the word Isaiah used for the canopy of protection, *ḥuppâ,* likely refers to the marriage chamber set up for privacy for a bride and groom on their wedding night. The word he used for shelter would have been known to the Jewish people as the booths set up during the Feast of Tabernacles (also called the Feast of Booths or Sukkot) that had a water-drawing ceremony that symbolized the coming of the Holy Spirit with the Messiah.[8] According to these verses, the Branch of the Lord has claimed you as His bride, and you will always be protected by the power of almighty God and guarded by the Holy Spirit—no matter what comes your way.

Have you ever felt this cherished and protected by God? Write about it here:

Now, read through the New Testament fulfillment of Isaiah 4:2–6 in Hebrews 10:1–14.

Did you notice how the old laws regarding sacrifice and sin were replaced with the single sacrifice of Christ?

Continue reading the next two verses (Heb. 10:15–16). In addition to the sacrifice of Christ, how is God going to give you that refuge and cleansing promised in Isaiah?

READ 1 JOHN 1:7–9 IN THE MARGIN. Circle "cleanse," "forgive," and "all."

Because of the glorious "Branch of the LORD," your sin stains were washed clean and then you were sealed with the best "stain guard" you can imagine—the power of God Himself—the Holy Spirit!

WHAT'S THE POINT?

As Christ followers, we should be basking in the glorious Branch of the Lord. Since the atoning sacrifice of Jesus on the cross has already taken place, our lives should be set apart, protected from the outside influences of our times and culture. We belong in the beautiful shelter of the Most High.

List three areas of your life that are being influenced by things *not* associated with God, but rather by the temporary things of this world:

> But if we walk in the light, as he is in the light, we have fellowship with one another, and the blood of Jesus his Son cleanses us from all sin. If we say we have no sin, we deceive ourselves, and the truth is not in us. If we confess our sins, he is faithful and just to forgive us our sins and to cleanse us from all unrighteousness.
>
> 1 John 1:7–9

People who come into contact with Christians should be able to sense the Shekinah glory of God that surrounds us.

Are the three areas you listed above causing the shine of God in your life to be dimmed? Why or why not?

HOW DO WE USE IT?

Consider that when Isaiah spoke the words in today's passage, the consequences of the Jewish people were still to come, looming in the future. If they believed Isaiah's words, terrible things were going to happen to them, their families, their friends, their city, and their nation. The Jewish people had to wait through anguish and destruction in hopes of getting to see the Messiah.

Yet, here we sit, comfortably in Bible study, safe and loved, in the arms of Jesus. The "beautiful and glorious" work of Jesus has already washed us clean, set up the marriage tent, and surrounded us with the power of God, no matter what comes our way. Use the promises of this fulfilled prophecy to change your attitude and your focus. Do your best to shift your thoughts and words from anything negative to the incredible positives in your life as a child of God.

List three negative thoughts or words that enter your mind the most:

Next, choose some of the words, phrases, and concepts we learned by studying to-day's passage (such as: beautiful, glorious, pride and honor, holy, my life is recorded in heaven, washed, cleansed, surrounded by God, protected, sheltered) and write them over your negative thoughts or words.

This week, begin each day by remembering these awesome privileges and let them be your Shekinah glory to everyone who encounters you.

The Virgin Birth

ISAIAH 7:10–14

Begin with prayer for a revelation only God can give you. Read the passage from Isaiah, looking for prophecies that could relate to the Messiah, His reign, or His kingdom. Throughout this study, you should feel free to mark up your Bible as you read. You may find it helpful to use colored pencils or highlighters to track themes or certain language. Take your time. Dig in!

READ ISAIAH 7:10–14 IN YOUR BIBLE, MARKING AS ABOVE. Next, turn to Luke 1:26–35 and read about the angel Gabriel and the virgin named Mary. You can read Joseph's side of the story in Matthew 1:18–25.

If only it were this easy: see the prophecy in the Old Testament, find its match in the New Testament, and call it "done"! Whether Jesus was born of a virgin or born in the normal course of men and women is at the heart of the debate about whether Jesus was really the promised Messiah. We must dig a bit deeper to uncover whether Jesus really was the Son of *God*. If you wonder, as I did in my youth, whether Jesus was just a man, clearly an amazing speaker, charismatic and compelling, but still just a man, then this is where we must start dealing with your doubts about Jesus.

Do you believe Jesus was born of a virgin?

Yes   Not Sure   No

If you circled Not Sure or No, write about your doubts:

Believing Jesus is the Son of God and that He was sent here by God to redeem humankind are two of the most important truths God wants you to understand from the Bible. Most of the New Testament is directed at these two points. For me, believing Mary gave birth to Jesus while still a virgin was critical to my putting *all* of my faith in Christ. My steadfast faith began by accepting that Jesus was born of a virgin and is the Son of God Himself.

Simply reading the passage in Isaiah and then the accounts in the gospels of Matthew and Luke, however, did not convince me before I was saved and filled with the Holy Spirit. I figured Mary and Joseph were Jews who would have read the book of Isaiah over and over again in their lives. Isaiah was written more than six hundred years before Jesus was born. I thought there was plenty of time for these folks to make up a lie to cover Mary's unexpected pregnancy. The stories of angels only increased my suspicion. It sounded like a fairy tale to me.

Yet, as a brand-new Christian, sitting outside one morning with the Bible in my hands, I asked the question all defense lawyers must ask about their cases and clients *inside* their heads (even if never spoken out loud): What if it's true? Could it be true? As the breeze blew across my face, I looked around our yard and saw hummingbirds zipping around, stopping briefly at my neighbor's feeder. That's when it struck me: What if it *is* true? How *could* it be true? Deep in my soul I felt a nudge, and heard the lyrics of a song in my head: "All of creation . . . sing[s] of His glory."[9]

"Well, creation is how it *could* be true," I thought, "if God did create the entire universe and everything in it, those hummingbirds are pretty spectacular. I believe He did create men and women from the dust of this earth. So, I guess He *could* make Mary pregnant if He wanted to."

To accept this idea, you have to believe God created the earth, the stars, animals, and men and women. If you don't believe God created everything around you, then the idea of Mary becoming pregnant without the help of Joseph will remain a fairy tale to you, impossible to believe. However, if you believe in God, consider this: If God can speak all life into existence, then why couldn't He form a child in Mary's womb?

List five things on earth or in the universe that "wow" you and point you to God as Creator:

If God created these things you listed and *all* the plants, oceans, stars, animals, humans, and so on, couldn't He decide to create a pregnancy in a young woman?

Now that we've tackled my logic, let's take a look at why this prophecy in Isaiah 7 has been called "the most controversial of messianic prophecies."[10] There are several things at play in this passage that lead critics to deny the virgin birth. First, the passage toggles back and forth, between prophecies that are near in time and far in time, and in the use of singular and plural words. Second, some scholars assert that the word Isaiah used that has been translated as "virgin" could also be translated as "young woman" or found to mean a pubescent girl. Let's take a closer look at Isaiah chapter 7.

In chapter 7, Isaiah was speaking to Ahaz, the wicked king of Judah. Ahaz and the people of Judah were terrified because armies (including its "sister" nation, Israel) were coming against them to replace King Ahaz with Tabeel's son as king (v. 6). Judah was special because it held the line of King David and represented the Davidic covenant. It was this "Davidic covenant (2 Sam. 7:12–16; 1 Chron. 17:11–14) that led to the expectation of a future Messiah who would be a descendant of David. Therefore, if Ahaz and the entire royal house were to be destroyed, it would bring an end to the messianic hope."[11]

So, the threat to Judah at the time Isaiah spoke these words to Ahaz supports an interpretation that this is a messianic prophecy. Through Isaiah, God was assuring His people that He would keep His word—that a future King would rule who came from the line of David (as Jesus does; see the genealogy of Jesus in Luke 3:23–38). He'd already made the promise and He sent Isaiah to tell them how He would fulfill it.

How can you be assured that God will keep His promises?

Just before Isaiah made the virgin birth prediction, he described an army that was poised to usurp Ahaz as king of Judah; Ahaz the king and the people of Judah were terrified. God told Isaiah to take his own son with him to speak to Ahaz (by the way, that son of Isaiah had a name that means "a remnant shall return") and tell Ahaz to calm down, stop fearing, and that the fall of Judah "shall not stand, and it shall not come to pass" (see Isa. 7:3–7).

Next, God told Ahaz, "If you will not believe, you surely shall not last" (v. 9 NASB). Because our almighty Father is so patient and filled with mercy, He told Ahaz that he could ask for a sign to destroy his unbelief. God even said to "let it be deep as Sheol or high as heaven" (v. 11). In other words, Ahaz could ask for *anything* as a sign.

What did Ahaz do? He refused as if he was religious enough to be offended, when he clearly was not; he worshiped other gods and even sacrificed at least one of his children (see 2 Kings 16:3 and 2 Chron. 28:3). One commentator put it this way: "Pious though his words sound, Ahaz is doing the devil's work of quoting Scripture for his own purposes and thereby displaying himself as the dogmatic unbeliever."[12]

So there was God, trying to assuage the fears of His people, going so far as to offer this pathetic king *anything* in terms of a miraculous sign, and the man refused to ask! What happened next? Isaiah addressed the whole house of David and then spoke the prophecy regarding the virgin birth. The words used here shift from addressing Ahaz in the singular to the plural form meant to address all of Judah, the whole "house of David."

The tension-packed scene, combined with God's offer to produce a sign as deep as hell or as high as heaven, lends support to the interpretation that this is, in fact, a statement about the *virgin* birth of the Messiah. A miracle. Something never before seen on earth—or since. A sign as high as heaven. A divine pregnancy. God with us.

If God gave you permission to ask for a sign (*any* sign) from Him, what would you ask of Him? Why?

The next big "problem" with the passage is that upon first reading it can appear to mean that the sign would occur in a short time, not six hundred years later! However, this pattern of combining both a "near" and a "far" prophecy was common in Isaiah. Most scholars agree there was both a "long-term prophecy" and a "short-term prophecy" in this passage. For a thorough and very interesting discussion of these "near" and "far" prophecies, pick up *The Moody Handbook of Messianic Prophecy*, and you can study how Isaiah's own sons were used as signs in the "near" prophecies and why Jesus was the "far" prophecy.[13]

Finally, one of the reasons this prophecy is so controversial is because, as we mentioned, the word Isaiah used for "virgin" could mean other things. Some critics claim the Hebrew word, "*alma* must mean 'young woman' and that *betula* is the technical word for 'virgin'."[14] However, early pre-Christian translations (the Septuagint) translated *almah* or *alma* to the Greek word *parthenos*, which means virgin in the sense that we understand it today.[15] In addition, a study of the use of these words throughout the Bible leads to a strong argument that using this word *alma* means virgin.

In every other situation where this word is used in the Bible, it either has a neutral meaning or it means virgin (not young woman). There is no place in your Bible where this same word was used to describe someone who was not a virgin.[16]

That's enough proof for me. How about you? Where are you now on the question at the beginning of today's lesson—do you believe in the virgin birth of Jesus? Is your answer the same or different now?

Next, let's deal quickly with the fact that Mary and Joseph did not call the baby "Immanuel" as the prophet Isaiah foretold. The name "Immanuel" in Hebrew means "God with us." Isaiah was pointing out that the child, who would be born of a virgin, was going to be God, walking and living among us . . . *with* us. Two chapters later, Isaiah also said our Savior would be born a child and called "Wonderful Counselor, Mighty God, Everlasting Father, Prince of Peace" (Isa. 9:6). These terms Isaiah used were describing who Jesus would be to us—His nature, not His literal name. Also, note that in Hebrew, Jesus is "Yeshua," which means "to deliver, to rescue."

What are some of your favorite names or attributes of God? List them here:

WHAT'S THE POINT?

How can a change in your thinking about whether Mary was a virgin or a teen caught in an early pregnancy impact your life today? It can change *everything!*

If Jesus was created in Mary's womb by God Himself, then Jesus really was who He claimed to be, and the Bible is true. Absolute truth.

When I was still wrestling with skepticism as a new believer, as I studied Isaiah, I came to the conclusion that whether I continued to put my faith in Jesus, or began to turn away from my newly found faith, hinged on this one point: Did I believe God created the heavens and earth?

Do you?

If yes, then you must admit everything else in the Bible *could* be true. What if it *is* true?! This outrageous thought fueled my Bible study for most of the next year in my faith journey. I kept studying because I truly believed there was a God, somewhere, who created the world I lived in every day. If *that* was true, then I had to submit my mind to the idea that these other outlandish and miraculous events described in my Bible are true as well.

Is anything holding you back from putting your full faith and confidence in the Bible?

How often do you use Scripture to guide your life? Would you like to use it more?

HOW DO WE USE IT?

The old Nike slogan comes to mind: Just Do It! Using the prophecy of the virgin birth in your life means setting aside human limits of reason. Putting your faith in Jesus as the Son of God Himself means putting your faith in the truth of Scripture. In order to use the power of Scripture in your life, you simply must get the content in your head so that it can impact your heart.

Do you enjoy reading your Bible? (It's okay to be honest!)

Yes   Sometimes   Not Really   No

If you answered Not Really or No, may I encourage you to explore other options? I often work with adults who do not enjoy reading. My husband does not read. He hates to read. He loves music, television, and movies. So he has to find other ways to get Scripture into his heart. You might need to try different things to get to a place where Scripture is accessible in your life. Scripture is available on audio, Christian content is accessible by radio, online, podcasts, and so on. It's totally okay (and this study might be very hard for you; I'll be praying for you; try getting a "study buddy" and take turns reading it out loud).

For to Us a Child Is Born

ISAIAH 9:1–11

Pray for discipline to keep going! Read the passage from Isaiah, looking for prophecies that could relate to the Messiah, His reign, or His kingdom. You may find it helpful to use colored pencils or highlighters to track themes or certain language. Take your time. Dig in!

READ AND MARK UP ISAIAH 9:1-11. Next, read Matthew 4:12–17 and see how Matthew ties this prophecy to Jesus.

While the virgin birth prophecy is known as one of the most controversial, Isaiah 9:6–7 is "one of the most famous passages in the entire book, [which] answers these hopes and dreams of the world, for it predicts a perfect ruler who will rule forever and ever over a prosperous and peaceful realm."[17]

Isaiah continued in his theme of darkness into light in the opening of this chapter. In chapters 7 and 8, Isaiah predicted Judah's destruction and doom. Here, he shifted to give them hope. The land of Zebulun and Naphtali were in the region of Galilee and were the hardest hit when Assyria invaded. This desolate land would be the first to see "the light," first to experience joy such as in harvesttimes or military victory, first to experience "the yoke of his burden, and the staff for his shoulder, the rod of his oppressor . . . broken as on the day of Midian" (Isa. 9:4), which was a great victory that the Jewish people knew came only from God.

Jesus began His public ministry in Galilee, and performed His first recorded miracle there, the wedding in Cana where He turned water into wine (John 2:1–11). Jesus began gathering His disciples in Galilee by the sea, and He began healing the sick there (Matt. 4:18–25)—so much so that "great crowds followed him from Galilee" (v. 25).

Which miracle that Jesus performed do you think gives the best proof that He is the Messiah? Explain why you picked that miracle as your best proof.

Which miracle touches your heart the most?

Isaiah 7 also continued to predict that a miraculous child would be born and would bring the glorious reign expected by the Jewish people and associated with the coming Messiah. "Expositors of all types (both critical and conservative) have connected the child in chap. 7 with the one is chap. 9."[18] This passage also "declared both the humanity ('a Child is born') and the deity ('a Son is given') of the Lord Jesus Christ."[19] Also, a child will be born "for" us and a child will be given "to" us.

You can see these same words used in Luke 2:11–12: "For unto you is born this day in the city of David a Savior, who is Christ the Lord. And this will be a sign for you: you will find a baby wrapped in swaddling cloths and lying in a manger," and in John 3:16: "For God so loved the world, that he gave his only Son, that whoever believes in him should not perish but have eternal life."

Individuals who do not want to give this passage messianic meaning claim that Isaiah was describing King Hezekiah, and assert that Hezekiah simply didn't live up to these grand pronouncements. Others assert this prophecy is another one of Isaiah's "both" prophecies—there is one near (Hezekiah) and one far (Jesus) in this single prophecy passage. Most scholars, however, agree that Isaiah 9:1–7 is a messianic prophecy.

There is also some argument about the words "Wonderful Counselor, Mighty God, Everlasting Father, Prince of Peace." Some assert this is the *Hebrew name* to be given the child. But the majority of Christian scholars claim these are descriptions referring to *the nature* of the child to be born.[20]

What do you think? Do you think these words represent the name(s) of Jesus, or do you think these words are meant to describe the nature of the One who was to come? Did you notice that each one of these words has a human element *and* a divine or eternal element?

Let's jump in with the scholars and take a look at each of these these words.

Wonderful Counselor (pele' yoetz): the word *pele'* is most often used in the Bible to describe the miraculous acts of God. It is often used to describe the supernatural. It's not the "this dinner was *wonderful*" word. It's more "this is one of the seven *wonders* of the world" word. "Counselor" today usually means someone who gives advice, but *yoetz* means to serve as an advisor who leads and helps or has the power to execute wise plans. It is the use of the word, *pele'*, however, that asserts the deity of the child.[21]

Mighty God ('el gibbor): El is the common word for God in the Hebrew Bible. Immanu*el* is God with us. *El Shaddai* is God Almighty. *El olam* is God the eternal. The word *gibbor* means mighty and is also often used to reference God. The word can refer to a powerful warrior or valiant military hero. Some critics claim this phrase means that the child will be a godlike warrior for the nation. There is no debate, however, that the use of *El* is a reference to deity. It is Isaiah's use of this same phrase in chapter 10 that closes the debate for me. In just a few more sentences, Isaiah used this same combination (*el gibbor*) to describe God Himself: "A remnant will return, the remnant of Jacob, to the *mighty God*" (Isa. 10:21).[22]

Everlasting Father (abi ad): it was common in Old Testament times for the king of a nation to call himself the "father" of the people in his country. The phrase used here, however, could be better translated as "the father of eternity." Jews also considered the word *abi* to mean "originator" or "source." One commentator stated, "If you want anything eternal, you must get it from Jesus Christ; He is the 'Father of eternity.'"[23]

Prince of Peace (sar shalom): just like the word "wonderful" used above, the word "peace" as we use it today is simply not enough to describe the true meaning of what Isaiah spoke. "The English word 'peace' only partially reflects the meaning of *šalom.* The word involves putting back together what had been divided. Thus it speaks of much more than merely the absence of hostilities."[24]

You may also recall that in the final words of Jesus before His crucifixion, and after His resurrection, Jesus spoke peace over the apostles (John 14; 20). In sum, Jesus came to earth as this child to offer peace between God and the human race, fixing what was broken.

We can conclude that the words themselves are the best argument for the conclusion that Isaiah was describing the nature of the Messiah, Jesus Christ.

What do you most often call God when you pray? Do you use words like those above to describe Him? What are your favorite names for God?

WHAT'S THE POINT?

We simply cannot exaggerate anything about our God. It's impossible. He turns light into darkness. He is the Father of eternity. He is mighty. He brings peace. He counsels us. When we pause to ponder the absolute wonder of God, our minds usually cannot keep up! He's too much. Too much of everything our minds can conjure up. Perfection and power. Holy and just. This is the child Isaiah spoke of. This is our Jesus!

What does this have to do with you? Go back to the last sentence in our passage today: "The *zeal* of the LORD of hosts will do this" (Isa. 9:7). Merriam-Webster defines zeal as "eagerness and ardent interest in pursuit of something: FERVOR."[25]

God was *eager* to fulfill the Davidic covenant. God was *ardent* about keeping His promise that someday a ruler would come from David's family lineage whose kingdom would be everlasting. God has *fervor* when it comes to fulfilling His Word.

The Bible has a lot to say about you as a child of God. There are so many promises to you in the Word of God. I think He's just as eager to fulfill His promises to His children as He was to send the Messiah. I think God is zealous for you!

What do you think? Do you think God is zealous for you? Explain why or why not.

HOW DO WE USE IT?

We can use what we learned in today's lesson by doing two things: (1) never lose our sense of awe and wonder about God and Jesus, and (2) trust that God will keep His promises. Isaiah spoke the words you studied today more than six hundred years before Jesus was born. As we continue to study words that Isaiah spoke that came true, my prayer is that your trust in God will grow with each lesson.

Today, spend some time journaling about these two life applications:

How can I make sure my awe and wonder about God stays fresh?

In what area of my life do I need to develop more trust in God?

The Root of Jesse

ISAIAH 11:1–10

Praise God, because this is the last day of heavy study this week. I promise not all your homework will be this long! Read the passage from Isaiah, looking for prophecies that could relate to the Messiah, His reign, or His kingdom. You may find it helpful to use colored pencils or highlighters to track themes or certain language and mark up your Bible as you read. Take your time. He is worthy of the work!

READ AND MARK ISAIAH 11:1–10 IN YOUR BIBLE. Now, don't panic, but turn to Matthew 1 or Luke 3 and scan the genealogy of Christ. No need to memorize it, but just appreciate that both Matthew and Luke took the time to track the ancestry of Christ without the help of the internet to demonstrate how Jesus was born from the line of David.

Next, read Romans 15:8–9, 12 to see how the apostle Paul demonstrates how Christ fulfilled Isaiah 11.

Today we are studying the final prediction in Isaiah's three-part prophecy regarding the birth and reign of the Messiah. Isaiah told us of the virgin birth (Day Two), the divine King (Day Three), and in chapter 11, the awesome ruler who would fulfill the Davidic covenant and restore creation. In chapter 11, Isaiah was no longer speaking of who was coming, but of *how* the Messiah will rule the earth. Isaiah was no longer waiting for the Messiah to come, but announcing His kingdom's glory!

Matthew, Luke, John, and Paul all wrote about Jesus and the fulfillment of Isaiah 11. You can read Matthew 3:16 and John 1:32 in the margin regarding how the Holy Spirit descended on Jesus.

In fact, Paul *specifically* stated that Christ became a servant "in order to confirm the promises given to the patriarchs," and linking Jesus as "the root of Jesse" and the statement "a signal for the peoples—of him shall the nations inquire" meant that salvation through Jesus should extend to the Gentiles (non-Jewish people). See Romans 15:8–12. I love what Paul wrote just after he linked the prophecies in Isaiah with Jesus:

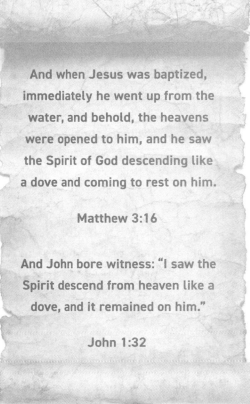

And when Jesus was baptized, immediately he went up from the water, and behold, the heavens were opened to him, and he saw the Spirit of God descending like a dove and coming to rest on him.

Matthew 3:16

And John bore witness: "I saw the Spirit descend from heaven like a dove, and it remained on him."

John 1:32

> May the God of hope fill you with all joy
> and peace in believing,
> so that by the power of the Holy Spirit you
> may abound in hope. (Rom. 15:13)

On first reading, and in today's culture, these words "hope" and "joy" and "peace" take on little meaning. When linked with Scripture, and in context of what Paul was saying, I think "by the power of the Holy Spirit you may abound in hope" means that the "Spirit of the Lord" from Isaiah 11:2 can *and* will fill you with:

the Spirit of wisdom and understanding,

the Spirit of counsel and might,

the Spirit of knowledge and the fear of the Lord.

And when that happens, when the Spirit of the Lord comes upon you with the gift of the Holy Spirit, the same Holy Spirit that descended upon Jesus descends on you and verse 3 is the result: "And [her] delight shall be in the fear of the LORD."

Please know that "fear" here means something like "reverence." Sweet sister, hope can only "abound" in a life whose delight is in her reverence of the Lord God Almighty. Peace and joy only fill you when Jesus is your delight and the Holy Spirit has come upon you. It's the only way.

On a scale of 1–10 (10 being high), where would you rate your "delight" in reverence for the Lord? Circle one:

1   2   3   4   5   6   7   8   9   10

Take a few minutes and brainstorm ideas for how you could increase your delight in the Lord:

How often do you think you experience wisdom, knowledge, counsel, and might from the Lord? Circle one (10 being often):

1   2   3   4   5   6   7   8   9   10

The ups and downs of this life tend to make us forget the moments when the Lord intervened in our lives. For some reason, all of human history shows that people forget what God has done for them when times are good, but then go running back to Him when trouble hits, often forgetting how He delivered them in the past. Let's try not to fall into that trap.

Journal about times in your life when God was clearly at work:

When Isaiah spoke the words in our passage today, he had just finished telling the people of Judah that they would be utterly destroyed, like a forest cut down and then burned. The dynasty of David would end. Just when it seemed all hope was lost, God reminded them who He is and that He would not forsake His promise. Thus, "a shoot from the stump of Jesse" would come. Commentators also suggest that this tiny "shoot" suggests the humble beginnings of Christ.[26]

Isn't it just like our God to show up when all seemed lost? From something that was supposed to be dead, life would sprout!

What seems "dead" in your life right now? What "sprouts" would give you hope that God has not forsaken you and this area of your life?

I believe there is very little doubt among Christians that Isaiah 11:1–5 portrayed Jesus Christ. There is, however, some debate regarding verses 6–9 and whether these descriptions are literal or imagery to depict the totally new nature of the earth under the reign of the Messiah. There are also debates about whether these words describe the time of Christ, the future "Millennial Age" (when Christ will rule the earth for a thousand years; see Rev. 20:1–7), or the times of the new heaven and new earth (see Rev. 21:1–7). Perhaps this is another one of Isaiah's dual prophecies, one that will take place both in the Millennial Age and in the new heaven and earth. Regardless of how you interpret these verses, no one disagrees that the fantastic times described represent a time when the curse of sin will be removed from mankind and creation.

Let's pause, however, on verse 9 for a moment because I think it may encourage someone reading this: "They shall not hurt or destroy in all my holy mountain; for the earth shall be full of the knowledge of the LORD as the waters cover the sea" (Isa. 11:9). Isaiah predicted that the earth would be filled with the "knowledge of the LORD" in a way that is huge and all-encompassing (as the waters cover the sea). Consider this:

> The Hebrew language does not recognize any distinction between knowledge that is an accumulation of information and knowledge that is personal acquaintance. For the Hebrews, all true knowledge is based on experience. Therefore, when the prophet speaks here about "knowledge of the LORD," he is not speaking primarily of knowledge *about* the Lord but of insight into reality born of a close and intimate relationship with him. The Messiah will make it possible for all people to know God intimately (emphasis in original).[27]

If your delight in the Lord is not as high as you'd like it to be, there's hope in Isaiah's prediction. Knowledge of the Lord comes from the Messiah—and He's already been here. You already believe in Him. Thus, you *can* know God intimately. I think this is one of Isaiah's dual prophecies. Both now and in the era of the new heaven and new earth, all people *can* know God intimately because the Messiah brought peace between His believers and God. This is both a "now" and "not yet" prophecy.

Finally, consider verse 10 as you ponder how the gospel has spread throughout the earth. Are the nations turning to the "root of Jesse"? Is Jesus a sign for all people? Do you think that Jesus' place seated at the right hand of the Father is glorious in heaven? My mind says "true," "true," and "true!"

For my fellow word "geeks," isn't it interesting that Isaiah switched the word from "shoot" to "root"? It becomes like the chicken or the egg conundrum. Which is it, a shoot or the root? How can this prediction of a coming ruler be *both*? It can only be both if these verses reference Jesus. Remember, He is the Father of eternity (Isa. 9:6). He existed before the formation of the world (see John 1:1–5). Jesus can be both, the root of the line of David—in His deity—and the shoot rising from the stump of Jesse—in His human form, Jesus.

WHAT'S THE POINT?

Even when devastating things happen to us, God can bring up a shoot of life, something new and good, out of our dreadful circumstances. Even when it looks like God is far away from us or our problems, He is working behind the scenes to bring us into our future glory. This life is only temporary. Another time is coming. God has promised us, through the predictions in Isaiah, and others, that there *will* be a day when He will rule this earth again and everything will be beautiful and in harmony with Him.

Allow the prophecies of Christ to shift your focus away from yourself and your life to those suffering around you with no knowledge of the Messiah. Let this knowledge of fulfilled prophecy make you bold for Christ's sake. Tell others that God always keeps His promises! Trust Him with all your heart and soul and step out in faith.

HOW DO WE USE IT?

Keep these promises near the front of your mind. Focus on them each day. Let the Word of God renew your mind. Begin each day remembering that everything you see around you, *and* everyone you encounter, is under the curse of sin. However, then shift your heart to the new world that is coming to all who believe in Christ, the Messiah.

How can you point others to the "shoot of Jesse," the Branch of the Lord? List at least three ways here:

Find three verses that encourage you to keep your mind focused on the eternal promises of God and list them here:

Spend time today meditating on these and be encouraged!

Review, Reflect, and Pray

Now that you've studied "the Book of Immanuel," do you think God kept what scholars call the Davidic covenant? Turn back to the beginning of Week One to read 2 Samuel 7:12–16 again.

Write whether you believe God kept His promise to David and why or why not:

Go back through the lessons and highlight the prophecies that had the most impact on you this week. Write the "address" of those prophecies here ("address" example: Isaiah 26:3):

Go back through the lessons and put a big question mark in the margin beside anything that you still have questions or doubts about, or where you want to learn more.

Write a prayer to God thanking Him for keeping His promises:

Week One:
The Savior Is Coming

GROUP DISCUSSION OR REFLECTION QUESTIONS

1. Do you feel sheltered and protected by God? If yes, describe when and how. If not, explain why not.

2. Do you struggle to stay positive, shining the light of Jesus, throughout your day? If yes, what can you do to keep yourself from sliding into negativity?

3. Do you claim the Bible as true? Does it hold authority and guidance over your life?

4. What doubts do you have that the Bible is true?

5. Brainstorm some ideas for how to get more Scripture into your head and heart.

6. What's the most awe-inspiring thing God has ever done in your life?

7. Describe a time when you struggled to see God working in your life.

8. Share your favorite promise from God or one that is especially meaningful to you today.

The Savior Will Conquer Sin and Death

For many of us, our most painful memories or our greatest fears revolve around death. Thoughts about the death of a loved one or our own death can fill our minds with pain and dread. Death remains a problem that is common to all people. It is a fact of life. Everything on this earth dies.

The cry of our heart is "Why?!" Why does everything and everyone have to die?

The answer is sin. Sin entered the world God created for us. Because God is perfect and holy, sin created separation between people and God. Because God is merciful, He created a way for that separation to be fixed. He cannot set His justice aside, however, and so God would require "lifeblood" as a consequence of sin. Perhaps you've heard it said this way: "The wages of sin is death" (Rom. 6:23). Because God is both holy and just, there had to be a penalty for sin.

Beginning with Abraham, God required a sacrifice of blood for the forgiveness of sins. For hundreds of years, the Jewish people sacrificed animals as sin offerings. Even though God's presence was with the Jewish people, He kept a veil between

them and had them perform the sacrifice of "lifeblood" for the forgiveness of sins.

When Jesus died on the cross, He declared, "It is finished!" (John 19:30), and the veil that separated God from people tore—from the top to the bottom (Mark 15:38)! This veil was a physical object, made with fabric and hanging in the temple's holy of holies. Only the high priest could enter this sacred space, and then only once a year. We'll read in Day One about a "veil" over one's heart.

Yet, dying on a Roman cross was not how the Jewish people had pictured the coming Messiah. They believed He would be a magnificent ruler over an Israel free of Roman rule, restoring God's people to glory. Jesus did that, but not in the way people expected Him to.

Thus, the verses we'll read about a stumbling block, a costly cornerstone, something that would shame the wise men of the Jewish people, came true. Jesus fulfilled the Scriptures in a way that confused them and caused them to reject Him, stumbling on their own pride and self-sufficiency.

Self-sufficiency and works-based favor are not from God. These notions are lies formed by the enemy to keep us running ragged and far from God. When our hearts are turned toward ourselves or others to fix our problems (sin or otherwise), we are not seeking God. We are not putting our faith in the God of heaven and earth. We are stumbling. We are separated.

Even so—the truth remains—Jesus swallowed death for all time for those who put their faith in His atoning work on the cross. It is, indeed, finished!

He Will Swallow Up Death for All Time

ISAIAH 25:6–9

Before you begin, ask God to give you eyes to see, ears to hear, and a heart to accept what He wants to teach you through the Scriptures today. Mark up the passage from Isaiah, looking for prophecies that relate to the Messiah, His reign, or His kingdom. You may find it helpful to use colored pencils or highlighters to track themes or certain language. Take your time. Dig in!

READ AND MARK UP ISAIAH 25:6–9 IN YOUR BIBLE. Next, read 1 Corinthians 15:54–57 where Paul preaches about the mortal putting on immortality in these often-quoted verses. Fill in the blanks starting with verse 55:

O death, _____ ___ ____ _____? O death, _____ ___ ____ _____? The sting of death is sin, and the power of sin is the law. But thanks be to _____ who gives ____ the victory through ____ ____ _____ _____.

Chapters 13–39 as a whole in Isaiah is considered the Woe of Nations, but in the midst of these dark judgments are words of hope and praise. Isaiah 25 opens in a song of praise with this verse: "O LORD, you are my God; I will exalt you; I will praise your name, for you have done wonderful things, plans formed of old, faithful and sure" (v. 1). From the day sin entered our world and created that veil of separation between humans and God, He had a plan to save us. Those same plans involve a day promised in our future when God will wipe the tears from our eyes (Rev. 21:4).

The Hebrew word for swallowed up "gives the picture of an overwhelming defeat of death, like the earth swallowing up the enemies of God."[1] This prophecy is another near and far, current and yet to come, prophecy. Isaiah 25:6–9 speaks of the work of the Messiah: a lavish feast for *all* people, because the veil of death covering *all* people and nations will be removed.

Read 2 Corinthians 3:12–17. What happened to the veil?

Could you or I remove the veil on our own? What's the only way the veil could be taken away?

What comes along with the Spirit of the Lord in v. 17?

In the temple in Jerusalem, a curtain separated the Holy Place (where God Himself dwelt among the people, and sometimes called the holy of holies) and the priests who served in the temple. Only the high priest, once a year, could go beyond that curtain, and only on the Day of Atonement (see Lev. 16). This curtain was described in Exodus 26:33–34: "And you shall hang the veil from the clasps,

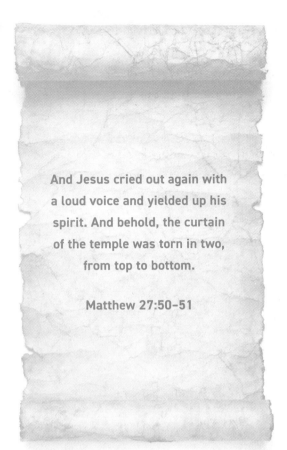

And Jesus cried out again with a loud voice and yielded up his spirit. And behold, the curtain of the temple was torn in two, from top to bottom.

Matthew 27:50–51

and bring the ark of the testimony in there within the veil. And the veil shall separate for you the Holy Place from the *Most* Holy. You shall put the mercy seat on the ark of the testimony in the Most Holy Place" (Ex. 26:33–34).

READ MATTHEW 27:50–51 IN THE MARGIN.

When Jesus gave up His life for us, that curtain was torn, and it is significant that it was torn from the top to the bottom. No longer was there a separation between God and His people. Jesus was the final sacrifice that atoned for *all* sin and death. The Day of Atonement had finally come once and for all. The veil was removed.

Do you feel like you are worthy to enter into the *Most* Holy place? What makes you feel like you do not belong in the presence of God?

Sister, we may not be worthy, but Jesus is! He has been presented to the Ancient of Days and deemed worthy:

I saw in the night visions,
and behold, with the clouds of heaven
there came one like a son of man,
and he came to the Ancient of Days
and was presented before him.

And to him was given dominion
and glory and a kingdom,
that all peoples, nations, and languages
should serve him;
his dominion is an everlasting dominion,
which shall not pass away,
and his kingdom one
that shall not be destroyed. (Dan. 7:13–14)

Repeat after me and say it out loud: Because *Jesus* is worthy, *I am deemed worthy.* I can enter the very presence of the Ancient of Days because Jesus removed the veil for me.

Let's look at one more famous scene in the Gospels: just before Jesus raised Lazarus from the dead, He very clearly stated that everyone who lives and believes in Him shall never die.

Read John 11:25–26. Write the question Jesus asks, which is the most important question of all time:

Do you? Do you believe it? Or, are you *hoping* it's true?

Merriam-Webster defines "believe" as "to accept something as true, genuine, or real."[2] On the other hand, "hope" is defined as "to cherish a desire with anticipation: to want something to happen or be true."[3] Hope can also be defined, however, as a transitive verb: "to desire *with expectation* of obtainment or fulfillment;" or "to expect with confidence: trust."[4] So, as long as your "hoping" is filled with *expectation* of eternal life because you trust in Jesus, then death has lost its sting over you!

The "not yet" part of Isaiah 25:6–9 is paralleled in Revelation 7 and 21.

In your Bible, circle every time the verses in Isaiah 25:6–9 use the word "all."

How many did you circle? _____

Jesus is for *everyone*. His banquet feast is open for *all* who believe in Him. At some point, all nations will recognize Jesus as the King of kings. When that happens, God will end our suffering, wiping every tear from our eyes. When God's kingdom finally comes, "death shall be no more, neither shall there be mourning, nor crying, nor pain anymore, for the former things have passed away" (Rev. 21:4).

WHAT'S THE POINT?

Jesus ended death for *all* who believe in Him. In the future, He will abolish death for all of creation, for all time. It's a glorious prophecy. With all the fulfilled prophecies piling up in your head (and hopefully in your heart too), is it difficult to believe in the new heaven and new earth that are foretold in the Scriptures? Or, is your hope filled with expectation?

If you're still struggling, I get it. Sometimes, this life is so tough that even the anticipation of the second coming of Christ is not enough to lift our chin. In the throes of grief, the hope of heaven is sometimes too far away. Even Martha, Lazarus's sister, who stated clearly she believed in the resurrection (not all Jews did) was not comforted by a future resurrection when her brother died. She ran out to Jesus essentially crying, "Why didn't you come?! Why didn't you stop this from happening? I know You could have. Why didn't You?" (see John 11).

Have you ever wanted to ask God those same questions? Write about those questions:

I sure did, and still do sometimes. My list grows longer each year. Even so, my hope remains in our God who keeps His promises. Someday, we will mourn no more. Never. Ever. Again.

HOW DO WE USE IT?

I love this verse in Corinthians, which comes shortly after the verses you studied today: "Therefore, my beloved [sisters], be steadfast, immovable, always abounding in the work of the Lord, knowing that in the Lord your labor is not in vain" (1 Cor. 15:58). We use our belief in Jesus and our hope in heaven as an anchor for our souls. We stand firm—even when life stinks—knowing that heaven is waiting, and a new heaven and new earth will be celebrated with a glorious feast for all who believe in Jesus.

Today, spend time searching the Scriptures. Find a verse that speaks of the power or promises of God to you. Make a screensaver image with that verse. Change your phone screen and your computer screen to your verse. Say it out loud before you get out of bed, before you start work, and every time you look at your phone.

Say Isaiah 25:9 out loud right now: "It will be said on that day, 'Behold, this is our God; we have waited for him, that he might save us. This is the LORD; we have waited for him; let us be glad and rejoice in his salvation.'"

Work on becoming steadfast and immovable in your faith by reading Scripture out loud.

Death Canceled by Costly Cornerstone

ISAIAH 28:14–21

Before you begin, ask God to give you eyes to see, ears to hear, and a heart to accept what He wants to teach you through the Scriptures today. Read the passage from Isaiah, marking up the verses as you look for prophecies that could relate to the Messiah, His reign, or His kingdom. You may find it helpful to use colored pencils or highlighters to track themes or certain language. Take your time. He is worthy of the work.

READ ISAIAH 28:14–21 IN YOUR BIBLE.

Next, read 1 Peter 2:1–8 and note how the prophecy was fulfilled.

Directed by the Holy Spirit, Peter spoke of "the stone that was rejected by you" in Acts 4:8–12. Paul also preached about the prophesied "stumbling stone" when he explained that God's "chosen people" now extended to the Gentiles who pursued righteousness by faith and not by works (Rom. 9:30–33).

God is referred to as a rock, a fortress, a stone, a foundation, and a cornerstone often throughout Scripture. This description was familiar to the Jewish people. There are several translations that refer to God or the Messiah as a "stone" in the Old Testament.[5]

I love how John Oswalt describes how God can be either a sanctuary or a stone:

> God's presence is the one inescapable fact of human life. We will encounter him in one way or another. Those who make a place for him find him to be the glue that holds everything together. Those who ignore him find their lives to be askew and cannot understand why. They have left out the most crucial factor in the equation of their lives, so that everything will always be unbalanced. The Lord God is either a sanctuary to dwell in or a stone to stumble over. Both Israel and Judah have chosen the latter way. Choosing to pay only ritual attention to God, they fall prey to every new fear that comes along. And being prey to their fears, they make all the wrong decisions.[6]

What fears are you falling prey to right now?

> The stone that the builders rejected
> has become the cornerstone.
> This is the Lord's doing;
> it is marvelous in our eyes.
> This is the day that the Lord
> has made;
> let us rejoice and be glad in it.
>
> Psalm 118:22–24

Has God been a sanctuary, or a stone to you? Write about those times:

READ PSALM 118:22–24 IN THE MARGIN.

In Matthew 21:33–41, Jesus tells an interesting parable about the owner of a vineyard and his tenants. Then He spoke of that cornerstone that was rejected in verses 42–44.

Write the question Jesus asks in verse 42:

For our families, friends, and neighbors who reject Christ, the message is terrifying. Even for believers, the message delivered to the Jewish people through Isaiah should cause us to pause and reflect.

Read the next few verses of Isaiah 28, verses 17–19. What covenant will be annulled (v. 18)?

Notice, however, that first your safety must be overwhelmed. You must, morning by morning, understand that death is coming for you.

If we are taking "refuge" in anything but God, it's a refuge of lies. For me, self-reliance and chasing after financial security are how I sometimes seek refuge or shelter in something other than the Lord. God will sweep such things out of our lives. He will overwhelm our flimsy shelters until we can only see Him. Then the ways that we've been falling into Satan's hands will be canceled. The constant returning of our souls to God Almighty will keep beating us down, morning by morning, day and night, until we surrender to His sovereignty. Nothing and no one will stand in God's place.

When Isaiah was speaking this message to Judah, the northern kingdom of Israel and the capital city of Samaria had already fallen to Assyria. The Assyrian army was brutal and all-encompassing in the way that it destroyed the cities it claimed. So, Isaiah 28 is filled with the coming destruction of the people, the land of Judah, and their beautiful Jerusalem.

Through Isaiah, God was warning His people that their reliance on human strength was not only misplaced, but would cause their destruction. God was angry that His people would turn to Egypt to save them from the Assyrians. Egypt was the only country near to Judah that had the wealth and resources to fight the Assyrians.

Didn't the Jewish people remember that they had been enslaved by Egypt for four hundred years? God's people were looking to the same Egypt who abused them and forced them into slave labor. Not even seeing their brothers and sisters in Israel fall to the Assyrians would turn them toward God. Rather, they kept running away from God, seeking shelter in the tangible wealth and resources of an enemy. God's people were trying to save themselves instead of relying on God.

Read Romans 9:30–33 and summarize the point in your own words:

Paul pointed out that the leaders of the Jewish people were "stumbling" over the gift and simplicity of salvation through faith in Jesus because they were clinging to their works-based traditions.

Isn't this still true today? I love the way Warren Wiersbe said it as he wrote about how God's prophets were rejected and mocked:

> Society today often takes a similar attitude toward God's servants and God's word. People are so intoxicated by intellectual pride that they laugh at the simple message of the gospel presented by humble witnesses (1 Cor. 1:18–31).[7]

WHAT'S THE POINT?

As we often find in God's Word, this ancient text still applies today; we sometimes try to save ourselves, especially when we are afraid. We tend to turn to something tangible to calm our nerves or fix problems.

In our human minds, it's hard to fault Judah. An army was coming. Soon. They sought help. Wouldn't you do the same?

What harm is coming to you right now? Sickness, relational problems, wayward kids, finances . . . and the list goes on. Write what you're afraid of or fighting through at this time:

Consider this statement: "God chides His people for a lack of trust in Himself. Egypt, He warns, cannot help. . . . The conflict between reason and faith is often a bitter one, chiefly because the reason is the reason of expediency [you need help *now*]. It is not actually reasonable because it leaves out the one all-important factor, the person of God."[8]

Rather than listen to Isaiah, the people listened to the leaders of Judah about seeking help from Egypt because "they advocated action in a terrible emergency. The impatience of the human heart was not satisfied by the admonition of the true prophet of God."[9]

Who are you listening to about your problems? Are they advocating action?

What are you impatient about? Are you seeking God's help for this problem, or pushing forward with something because it's action you can do yourself?

HOW DO WE USE IT?

We can learn from Judah's mistakes. We can look carefully at our lives and our relationship with God.

Take a few minutes to consider whether God is truly your refuge, your cornerstone, a foundation in your life. Write what comes to mind:

Sometimes, it feels like *God* becomes a stumbling block when we are trying to help ourselves. There are times when I get so busy that my quiet time, serving, or church service seem to be "in the way" of what I feel like I should be doing to solve my problems. There are weeks and months when I feel overwhelmed and end up irritated or edgy about taking the time to be with the Lord in the morning or serve at church. I don't like to admit that, but it's true sometimes. That edgy feeling about time with God or serving His kingdom should be a clue to me that I'm trying too hard to help myself instead of relying on God. Does that ever happen to you?

How could you turn to God to satisfy your heart in the midst of your problem?

The Wise Put to Shame

ISAIAH 29:13–24

In today's lesson, we have three prophecies in one passage. Buckle up, readers, you can do it! Remember, He is worthy of the effort.

The first prophecy is about how God's people would practice religion, but not truly worship Him. This prophecy was quoted by Jesus to the Pharisees. The second prophecy was that the Lord would do wonderful things among the people and put their wise men to shame. The final prophecy in today's lesson told us the Lord would make the deaf hear, the blind see, the meek find joy, and that the poor would exalt the Holy One of Israel. Is any of this sounding like Jesus to you? Now, remember, the words of Isaiah were written more than six hundred years before Jesus was born!

Let's dive in: before you begin, ask God to give *you* eyes to see, ears to hear, and a heart to accept what He wants to teach you through the Scriptures today. Read the passage from Isaiah, looking for prophecies that could relate to the Messiah, His reign, or His kingdom. You may find it helpful to use colored pencils or highlighters to track themes or certain language. Take your time.

READ ISAIAH 29:13–24 IN YOUR BIBLE.

Now read the scene where Jesus throws this prophecy in the face of the Jewish leaders in Matthew 15:1–9 (see also Mark 7:1–13).

I feel like Isaiah essentially told the Jewish people that they would experience something wonderful from the Lord, but it would be "upside down" or the opposite of what they might expect. What God would do for His people would stump even the wisest men and women.

The "near" prophecy was that God was about to allow the destruction of His people's nation and the temple so that their hearts would be turned back to Him. I'm a great example of how God will allow something horrible to happen so that a heart would turn to Him. Without losing our son, I'm not sure I would have ever come to know Jesus in the way that I do now. God used my shattered heart to make me see His love for me. It was devastating, but life-saving.

Have you ever experienced pain that drove you straight into the arms of God? (It could be something that happened to you either as a believer or before you were a Christian.) Explain how your pain led you closer to God:

The "far" prophecy related to Jesus and the wonderful work He would do. Isaiah told the Jewish people ahead of time so they would recognize Jesus when He came. But their hearts were far away from God and they missed it.

Sometimes I feel like I'm missing "it" as well. Life gets going, I tend to my family, do my job, go to church, serve and give . . . and yet, my life sometimes still feels as if I haven't quite grasped what this is all about. Like I'm missing something important.

I think this is because I am a task-based person. Set a task before me and I'll get it done. What's next? I'm not a vision-casting person. I'm not a dreamer. I'm not even a goal-setter. I tend to do what's in front of me, and even put off what can be done tomorrow. Give me a task *and* a deadline and I'm a happy girl!

So, comprehending God's vast universe and plans for humankind is beyond my normal operation. But prophecy tends to stop me in my tracks. When it's so clear to me, I begin to wonder how anyone missed the fact that Jesus is our Savior, our Messiah.

Isaiah told them they would stumble over what He was going to do. Isaiah told them the wise men would look foolish. The Jewish people were told that God would do wonderful things, like healing the deaf and blind. Yet, they could not see it when it happened.

Now, ponder this: the Jewish people weren't supposed to get it. If the people truly understood who Jesus was, then we wouldn't have a Savior. If the people hadn't cried out to crucify Jesus, Pontius Pilate would have set Him free (see John 19).

The consequence of sin entering into the world is death (see Gen. 3:19; 9:5). Tracking through the history between God and humankind, God required a living sacrifice to atone for sin. Over and over again, the Jewish people made sacrifices of blood for the forgiveness of sin.

Jesus was the only way to put a stop to the burden of sin on us. A perfect sacrifice, once and for all. Only God could design something that was both just and merciful—and confusing if you didn't understand the requirement of atonement for sin in the form of lifeblood.

On a scale of 1 to 10 (with 10 being highest), where would you rate your understanding of the atonement for sins that Jesus performed on the cross?

1   2   3   4   5   6   7   8   9   10

Are you still wondering why Jesus is the only way to heaven?

Yes   Yes, a little   No

Write what you would tell someone about: (a) why Jesus had to die on the cross, and (b) why Jesus is the only way to salvation and heaven.

Do you think *all* of your sins are fully forgiven forever? Why or why not?

I think we all have sins that we bring to the altar again and again, struggling to believe in full and final forgiveness through Jesus. Write about that struggle here:

Remember what Isaiah told us would happen when Jesus was in the midst of His children: "Jacob shall no more be ashamed, no more shall his face grow pale" (Isa. 29:22). Now substitute "I" for Jacob and "my" for his. Read it out loud.

Next, find a red marker and write "ONCE AND FOR ALL!" over the top of your sin struggles above. Take a moment to thank Jesus for His sacrificial love for you, His forgiveness, and His grace.

READ ZECHARIAH 3:8–10:

> "Hear now, O Joshua the high priest, you and your friends who sit before you, for they are men who are a sign: behold, I will bring my servant the Branch. For behold, on the stone that I have set before Joshua, on a single stone with seven eyes, I will engrave its inscription, declares the Lord of hosts, and I will remove the iniquity of this land in a *single* day. In that day, declares the Lord of hosts, every one of you will invite his neighbor to come under his vine and under his fig tree."

What did Isaiah call the Messiah in Isaiah 4:2?

What did Isaiah call the Messiah in Isaiah 28:16?

Jesus will remove the iniquity of His people in a _____ day. Once and for all.

Now, let's turn to the miracles of healing the deaf and blind. Just kidding! This homework day is long enough and we get to come back to the healings performed by Jesus next week when we study His ministry. We'll cover the healing of the blind in greater detail then.

WHAT'S THE POINT?

Sometimes, the way God works things out seems "wrong" or confusing to us. It's tough to be "wise" when it comes to God's sovereignty. We need to let God be God and accept that we may not understand or agree with the way this world works. Our role in life is to keep our focus on *worshiping* God instead of trying to *understand* God.

Life will feel a whole lot better if we stand firm on the atonement of Christ on the cross. If we can be steadfast in our belief that we are truly forgiven for all of our sins, the peace and joy of Jesus will surround us.

HOW DO WE USE IT?

We become more comfortable expressing our doubts and confusion to God. We open the lines of communication to these uncomfortable subjects. We tell God when we're struggling to worship Him through difficult circumstances. We tell God when shame begins to rear its ugly head about our past sins. Next, we sit still. We listen. We allow the Holy Spirit to guide us into all truth and bring to remembrance all that Jesus taught us (John 14–16).

We pray and allow the peace of God, which is beyond our comprehension, to guard our hearts and our minds in Christ Jesus (see Phil. 4:4–7). We shift our focus. Christian folks often quote Philippians 4:6 where we're told, "Do not be anxious about anything," but that leaves out the previous instruction ("Rejoice in the Lord always") and the last instruction (what we need need to focus our minds on).

READ PHILIPPIANS 4:8 IN THE MARGIN
and write the things we are supposed to be thinking about. I gave you the first letter of each word:

Whatever is

T _____

H _____

J _____

P _____

L _____

C _____

E _____

W _____ of P _____

Finally, [sisters], whatever is true, whatever is honorable, whatever is just, whatever is pure, whatever is lovely, whatever is commendable, if there is any excellence, if there is anything worthy of praise, think about these things.

Philippians 4:8

Take a few moments to dwell on these "whatevers."

The Teacher Is with You

ISAIAH 30:15–22

Try to picture Jesus sitting at your kitchen table. Can you see Him there? I think the series *The Chosen* has helped people put a "face" with Jesus and make people feel more connected to Him. Though the series takes some artistic liberties, it's well worth viewing. I know the actor's face is not the real face of Jesus, but I think the program could help you envision the loving heart of Jesus.

As you picture Jesus walking among us, ask God to give you eyes to see, ears to hear, and a heart to accept what He wants to teach you through the Scriptures today.

READ ISAIAH 30:15-22 IN YOUR BIBLE. As you've been doing, feel free to mark up the passage as you look for prophecies that could relate to the Messiah, His reign, or His kingdom. You may find it helpful to use colored pencils or highlighters to track themes or certain language. Take your time. He is worthy of the work.

Now read John 13:12–13. In His final teaching, during the Last Supper, Jesus confirmed Isaiah 30:20. Write how Jesus described Himself in John 13:13 below:

During the Last Supper, Jesus said, "You call me _____ and _____, and you are right, for so ___ ____."

It's important to note that the hope found in Isaiah 30:15–22 follows dire warnings. Read Isaiah 30:1–3. Instead of turning toward God in repentance and rest, the Jewish people would turn to Egypt to save them from the Assyrian army. In the same way, don't we try to fix things ourselves? How have you run to other things to help you instead of turning to God for help?

Let's pause and ponder these words from verse 15: returning and rest, quietness and trust. In this verse, "returning" can also be translated "repentance." Now let's go down to verse 18 and allow ourselves to perceive that God "waits to be gracious" to us; that Jesus exalted Himself "to show mercy" to us because "the LORD is a God of justice; blessed are all those who wait for him" (in v. 18). Dwell on the remarkable truth that it is God who calls *us*, not the other way around. *He* initiates salvation, reaching down to us—He is no false god who expects us to reach up to it, not another helper like "Egypt," and clearly not an armful of good works we rely on to earn our salvation.

READ ISAIAH 30:18 IN THE MARGIN.

How does it make you feel to know that almighty God, the Holy One of Israel, longs to be gracious to you, that He is waiting to show you compassion?

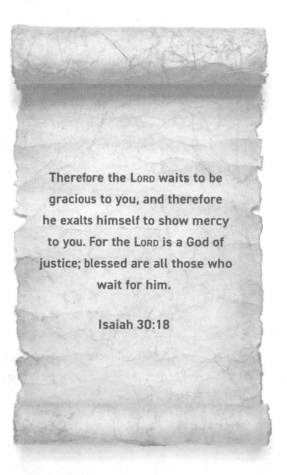

Therefore the LORD waits to be gracious to you, and therefore he exalts himself to show mercy to you. For the LORD is a God of justice; blessed are all those who wait for him.

Isaiah 30:18

When you cry out to God for help, check out this promise in verse 19: "You shall weep no more. He will surely be gracious to you at the sound of your cry. As soon as He hears it, He answers you."

As soon as you cry out to Jesus as your Savior and Lord, He will answer you—in returning (repentance) and rest, in quietness and trust. The peace of God will come to you. Go to Jesus and He will give you rest.

Isaiah told the people that, after a period of judgment, their Teacher would not hide Himself anymore, but they would see their Teacher with their eyes. Because of some confusing grammar choices in the original Hebrew text, there are three predominant views of who this "Teacher" is in this passage. The first theory is that "Teacher" refers to the prophets. The second theory is that "Teacher" refers to a king or Isaiah. The final theory is that "Teacher" is a "plural of majesty" that refers to God.[10]

I agree with the writer in Moody's *Handbook of Messianic Prophecy* that the third interpretation is the strongest. Neither the prophets, a king, nor Isaiah were hidden at the time these words were spoken or written (although the prophets were ignored). In addition, an early Jewish translation of Isaiah translated "Teacher" as Shekinah, which was usually used to describe an activity of God.[11] Shekinah or Shechinah is defined by Merriam-Webster as "the presence of God in the world as conceived in Jewish theology."[12]

The phrasing that comes next in Isaiah 30:21—"And your ears shall hear a word behind you, saying, 'This is the way, walk in it,' when you turn to the right or when you turn to the left"—would have been understood by the Jewish people to be like a shepherd leading his sheep. In that time, it was "quite common for a shepherd to guide and lead his flock from behind."[13]

Read John 10:1–15. Jesus called Himself the good shepherd. How does Jesus guide His sheep in this passage?

I love John 10:27–29 because Jesus spoke words of such promise and power.

Rest assured, sweet sister, the Teacher was in our midst and has called *you* His own and no one can separate you from Him. Find peace in the fact that the Father is greater than *all* things. Listen to your Shepherd's voice when He says, "This is the way, walk in it."

The gift of the Holy Spirit is the new covenant promise to all those who put their faith in Christ. The Holy Spirit will guide us into all truth, telling us which way to go. When you sense that voice in your spirit, listen to the direction the Holy Spirit is giving you. He will guide you. You need only to listen and take the next step.

What guidance are you listening for during this season of your life?

> "My sheep hear my voice, and I know them, and they follow me. I give them eternal life, and they will never perish, and no one will snatch them out of my hand. My Father, who has given them to me, is greater than all, and no one is able to snatch them out of the Father's hand."
>
> John 10:27–29

Can you give an example of when the Holy Spirit guided your steps?

When have you felt the rest offered by Jesus?

The final action in our passage often follows when someone turns to God. Idols and man-made things are seen for the little value they hold. Those things that draw you away from God (e.g., idols, self-sufficiency, wealth) can be set aside when you rest in the Lord and follow the Holy Spirit.

WHAT'S THE POINT?

Doing life without consulting God can lead to disaster. Self-sufficiency will not save us. Our only rest comes from repentance. God has never tried the "hidden ball trick" on people. He has told us many times, in many ways, that He alone holds our existence in His mighty hands.

Yet, even when we mess up, God longs to be gracious to us! God waits for us to return to Him. He is patiently waiting for us to discover His rest and provision instead of running around trying to solve everything ourselves.

He would like nothing better than to destroy our prideful striving and fearful fleeing. If we'll consult God and wait on Him, both our spiritual and physical needs will be met (see the rest of Isaiah 30 for the blessings that result from turning back to God).

HOW DO WE USE IT?

We need to take time to identify where, when, how, and why we go elsewhere to meet our needs before we consult God. We need to find those areas where we are walking by sight, not faith.

What problems are causing you the most worry or anxiety right now?

Are you putting your trust in any other things, institutions, people, and so on to help solve the problem? Have you been striving in self-sufficiency about this problem?

Have you enlisted a prayer team to help you with this problem? Who could you ask?

Or perhaps you might be like me—sometimes I hear God's voice clearly and still don't manage to follow His way or walk in His calling. Failure to follow is disobedience as sure as direct rebellion.

Is there some area of disobedience blocking the blessings God is waiting to give you?

Write a statement of repentance and at least one step you can take to move in the direction God desires:

Review, Reflect, and Pray

Today, take some time to imagine seeing God face to face. The veil of sin no longer separates you from God. You can experience His presence. Perhaps listen to the song "I Can Only Imagine" by MercyMe.

Set an alarm on your phone around lunchtime. Make it a reminder to seek God for all your plans.

Go back through the lessons and highlight the prophecies that had the most impact on you this week. Write the "address" of those prophecies here ("address" example: Isaiah 26:3):

Go back through the lessons and put a big question mark in the margin beside anything that you still have questions or doubts about, or where you want to learn more.

Write a prayer of repentance and rest, asking God to tell you "this is the way, walk in it." List the areas of your life where you need to let go of self-sufficiency.

Week Two:
The Savior Will Conquer
Sin and Death

GROUP DISCUSSION OR REFLECTION QUESTIONS

1. Do you struggle to feel the presence of God? How can you push through these times?

2. How often do past sins or regrets enter your mind? What could you do to set those forgiven sins aside for good?

3. Is Jesus as the *only* way to salvation still a bit of a stumbling block to you?

4. Can you explain salvation in your own words?

5. What are some ways you can run to God instead of running yourself ragged?

6. List what's troubling you on one side of a paper. On the other side, write the characteristics, attributes, or names of God. Next, draw an arrow through each worry and direct it to a characteristic or name of God.

7. Describe a time when you struggled with self-sufficiency. How did you overcome it?

8. Write one lesson the Teacher has taught you in this past year.

The Savior with Us

This week we'll begin our study of the specific acts of Jesus that were spoken more than six hundred years before those moments took place. We'll see how Jesus healed, how John the Baptist prepared the people for the coming Messiah, and how God would choose Jesus to be our gentle Savior.

Also, at this place in the book of Isaiah, we are coming to a major shift. As mentioned, scholars generally agree that chapters 1–39 relate to the judgment of the chosen people, and chapters 40–66 restore the hope of God's people that He would not abandon them, nor would He forsake them as His people. As Warren Wiersbe explains, "The Jewish rabbis have called Isaiah 40–66 'The Book of Consolation,' and they are right."[1]

This part of Isaiah can be further described as three sections: deliverance, chapters 40–48; the Suffering Servant, chapters 49–57; and the glorious consummation, chapters 58–66.[2] Of course, these divisions were not in the original scroll, but putting titles on the sections helps us better understand the structure of this part of Isaiah.

When we get to Day Four in this week's study, we'll come to the first of the "Servant Songs" in the book of Isaiah. Much of the book of Isaiah is considered

poetry, and certain sections have been identified as beautifully describing our Messiah. The Servant Songs are generally known as 42:1–7; 49:1–6; 50:1–11; and 52:13–53:12.[3]

Finally, keep in mind that Isaiah was speaking these words *before* Babylon was a world power, and before Judah fell into captivity. Our God plans ahead! He knew His people would need the second half of the message from Isaiah. The Jewish people probably felt let down, disappointed, discouraged—they'd completely lost their hope. But God will not leave them in this dark place.

It's the same for us—we need the *whole* Word of God to understand fully and be ministered to by God.

About this "Book of Consolation," John Oswalt said:

> The dominant idea here is that of the undeserved grace of God. This is what will motivate the people to trust God, just as was intimated in chapter 12. When God delivers his people without any deserving on their part, they will at last be willing to cast themselves on him without reservation. So if chapters 7–39 were about trust as the basis for servanthood, chapters 40–55 are about grace as the motive and the means of servanthood.[4]

Are you ready to study the grace of our God?

The Blind See,
The Lame Walk

ISAIAH 35:1–10

As you picture Jesus walking among us, ask God to give you eyes to see, ears to hear, and a heart to accept what He wants to teach you through the Scriptures today.

READ ISAIAH 35:1–10 IN YOUR BIBLE. Feel free to mark up the passage, as you look for prophecies that could relate to the Messiah, His reign, or His kingdom. You may find it helpful to use colored pencils or highlighters to track themes or certain language. Take your time. He is worthy of the work.

NEXT, READ MATTHEW 11:2–6.

What question did John the Baptist ask Jesus?

How did Jesus answer?

Throughout the Gospels, there are many accounts of Jesus healing people. Below is a list of Scriptures describing the miraculous healings performed by Jesus. Pick a few (or all of them) and read them today.

Matthew 9:1–8
Matthew 9:27–31
Matthew 12:22–23
Matthew 15:29–31
Mark 7:31–37
Mark 8:22–26

Mark 10:46–52
Luke 18:35–43
John 9:1–7
John 5:5–9
John 11:11–44

Isaiah 35 has it all—the glory of God, both spiritual and physical healing, and the restoration of this natural world to its previous splendor. Why? The answer is there in black and white: God will come to save you.

The English Standard Version of the Bible gives Isaiah 35 this chapter heading: "The Ransomed Shall Return." As you read this passage, you might be wondering whether this chapter relates to Christ's time on earth or if it's talking about eternity. I think it's both. That's the beauty of Isaiah's writing and our God's creativity and brilliance. He can do all things, including writing and preserving this passage of Scripture to encourage us toward heaven and embolden us to live in this present truth: we've been freed from captivity. As believers in Christ, we're already walking on the Highway of Holiness. We no longer have any barriers between us and God.

Do you sometimes feel as though there's a barrier between you and God? What is getting between you and God?

I heard this once from a pastor and it always strikes a chord with me: You are as close to God as *you* want to be.

It's true. You can choose to tackle every single hour of your day with God, or you can set Him to the side for Sundays only. Or, like I did for many years, you can turn your back on Him and the Helper. But it is *your* choice.

Hurts a bit, doesn't it? We like to pretend that those who seem to have a vibrant connection with God have entered into some uncommon, special relationship with Him. Like maybe God plays favorites—and perhaps I'm not one of them. Sound familiar?

It's a lie. If you've put your trust in Jesus for eternal life you are one of the redeemed. You've been ransomed. God went to such great lengths to rescue you. He left His majesty and perfection behind to come to this earth, was rejected, spat upon, beaten, and killed in a grisly manner. All for you.

After all of that, do you really think He'd stay aloof? Do you think such love could stand at a distance? Doesn't it make more sense that *you're* the one who puts distance between you?

Write your thoughts:

And if you've not yet made the decision to put your trust in Jesus, perhaps it's time for you to surrender your life to Him. He loves you so much. He's safe. You can trust Him. How can you do that? You can do it right here, right now. You can pray this prayer:

> *Father God, I know that I'm a sinner who needs a Savior. I believe Jesus died on the cross for the forgiveness of my sins, so that I can know You, God, and have eternal life. I believe Jesus is the Son of God and He died on the cross for my sins, and rose from the grave and now sits at the right hand of the Father. I want Jesus to be my Lord and Savior. Come into my life, Jesus. I put my faith in You and You alone. Amen!*

If you prayed that prayer for the first time, you just made the best decision of your life! Would you please email me at kim@kimaerickson.com and allow me to celebrate and pray over you? I'd love to know you've become a new creation!

Let's keep studying.

Isaiah 35 is a beacon of hope amid the judgment of Israel and Judah. Chapter 35 also is a "mirror" to chapter 30 (and our lesson in Week Two, Day Four). Isaiah 30 speaks of God's wrath against the arrogant nations. Isaiah 35 describes the future of the Lord's redeemed. Isaiah 30 explains what happens when we trust others, ourselves, or this world. Isaiah 35 describes what is in store for those who trust in the Lord. Glory awaits us! Doesn't it sound beautiful?

Write your favorite images from Isaiah 35 and explain why you like these:

Read Isaiah 35:2–4 again. Isaiah said, "They shall see the glory of the Lord, the majesty of our God." Historically speaking, the Jewish people would have recognized that a physical manifestation of God on this earth was "often accompanied by supernatural and miraculous signs."[5] When Jesus walked this earth, He certainly showed the people the glory of the Lord. Jesus strengthened the weak and feeble, healing everywhere He went. Also, the Gospels record Jesus telling people to "take courage," "do not be anxious," or "do not let your heart be afraid" several times.

Think back on some of the healing miracles of Jesus you looked up. How do these bring you confidence in Him? Which examples taught you something about Jesus?

Isaiah used a highway as a theme throughout his teachings (Isa.11:16; 19:23; 40:3; 62:10).[6] As Isaiah described the beauty of the restored land and redeemed people, he also told us, "The unclean shall not pass over [the highway]. It shall belong to those who walk on the way" (Isa. 35:8). Do you perceive this as exclusive? Judgmental? Narrow-minded? Or is this a wide-open six-lane highway for all who want to travel on it?

Jesus told us: "I am the way, and the truth, and the life. No one comes to the Father except through me" (John 14:6). I used to perceive the requirement of faith in Jesus for salvation to be exclusive. I rejected anyone's judgment of whether or not I was "clean" or "unclean." I did not understand the atonement. I did not understand the curse of sin and the need for Jesus. I thought it was about "holiness" in my behavior.

The Way of Holiness has *nothing* to do with your behavior. It has nothing to do with you at all. *Every* human is separated from God because of sin. No amount of good deeds could make God go back on His word that lifeblood would be required of every man and beast. Because of the penalty for sin—lifeblood—Jesus had to die on that cross. Otherwise, humankind would have remained captive to sin.

Jesus is not exclusive. Rather, Jesus is once and for *all*. It is finished (John 18:30).

Did you know that the law states a person has to *accept* a gift before ownership of the gift will transfer to the recipient? It's true. If I wanted to give you my diamond earrings, I couldn't do it legally unless you accepted my gift. Even if I left them on your doorstep, those earrings wouldn't become yours unless you accepted my gift. The gift of the forgiveness of sins through Jesus' sacrifice on the cross is the same. You must accept the gift of His sacrifice before it can become yours. On the other hand, if you let His gift sit there, or if you reject it, it can never become yours. The choice of accepting the gift is yours.

That's my lawyer explanation of how the atonement by Christ works for our salvation (and why it's not exclusive, but rather each person's own choice). Write how you could explain this to someone else. Try to use something familiar in your life and make a connection:

WHAT'S THE POINT?

Read John 9. Some of the Jewish people who were around when Jesus was healing were quite determined to discredit Him. The religious leaders needed something against Jesus. Look at the lengths they went to in this one example. The neighbors were talking about this man, blind from birth, who could now see. They went and talked to the Pharisees about it.

The Pharisees investigated and heard how Jesus healed the man. But they didn't stop by talking to the neighbors and the man. The Pharisees sought out the man's parents, who confirmed the man was their son and had been blind from birth, but the parents did not speak of Jesus healing their son because they were afraid of getting tossed out of the synagogue.

Consider this: if the blind man's story was a hoax, there would be proof. Somewhere along the way, someone would have spilled the beans if these healings were fake. The Pharisees would have uncovered something to show Jesus really didn't heal the people described in your Bible. Jesus did these things during a time when written history existed. Important events were recorded in written form.

Where are the documents disputing these miracles? Where is the proof Jesus *didn't* heal people? There are statements of disbelief, but no *evidence* to speak of. No fraud has been documented—only disbelief, a flat refusal to believe in Jesus.

Finally, consider what the formerly blind man told the Pharisees when the investigation circled back to him: "Never since the world began has it been heard that anyone opened the eyes of a man born blind. If this man were not from God, he could do nothing" (John 9:32–33).

The man had a point! There are examples of other kinds of healings in the Old Testament, but never healing the blind from birth.

I think this is the reason John wrote so much about this particular healing and the investigation that ensued. John was proving a point. The Pharisees *tried* to disprove the healing, but failed. The logical conclusion is that Jesus healed a man blind from birth. Thus, Jesus was who He claimed to be: the Messiah.

HOW DO WE USE IT?

We use the fact that Jesus healed these people as assurance for our minds and our faith. God really did come to save us. The Ancient of Days really did send His only Son to die in our place. Isaiah 35:10 says, "The ransomed of the LORD shall return and come to Zion with singing; everlasting joy shall be upon their heads; they shall obtain gladness and joy, and sorrow and sighing shall flee away." Read 1 Timothy 2:3–6 in the margin on the next page.

We rest on the blood of Jesus. We've been redeemed. Although we had been snatched away by sin, we've been ransomed by Jesus. He paid the price for us.

We are clean. We are on the Way of Holiness.

Notice that the Way of Holiness is described like a road. It's a journey! We have not arrived yet. But the descriptions of Zion and the restored earth *will* come someday. If we're standing firm in our faith in Jesus, our hope in heaven and eternal life can be firm and foremost in our mind. God kept His word about sin. God kept His word about the Savior. God will keep His word about a new heaven and a new earth where we will have everlasting joy and gladness, where our sorrow and sighing will flee away.

We use these assurances to keep our hearts and minds focused on God and His way. We set aside anxiety and worry because God always keeps His promises. He also puts His safeguards around us. Did you notice how that holy highway was described? Check it out: "It shall *belong* to those who walk on the way; *even if* they are fools, they *shall not* go astray" (Isa. 35:8).

Once you are on the path of Christ, you can't go wrong! Stand firm, God's guardrails won't fail.

> This is good, and it is pleasing in the sight of God our Savior, who desires all people to be saved and to come to the knowledge of the truth. For there is one God, and there is one mediator between God and men, the man Christ Jesus, who gave himself as a ransom for all, which is the testimony given at the proper time.
>
> 1 Timothy 2:3–6

The Voice of One Calling in the Wilderness

ISAIAH 40:1–8

Today you will study a prophecy that was included in all four gospels in nearly the same way—that John the Baptist was the voice crying out in the wilderness and preparing the way for the Messiah. As you consider this prophecy and the relationship between John the Baptist and Jesus, ask God for special insight through the Scriptures today. Begin by praising God for the fact that His Word lasts forever and will continue to give us hopeful expectation for what is yet to come.

READ ISAIAH 40:1–8 IN YOUR BIBLE. As always, I encourage you to mark up the passage. You may find it helpful to use colored pencils or highlighters to track themes or certain language. Take your time. He is worthy of the work.

Read Matthew's account of John the Baptist in Matthew 3:1–12 (you may want to also see Mark 1:1–8; Luke 3:1–6, 15–17; and John 1:6–8, 19–28).

Next, in the margin on the next page, read how Peter linked Isaiah 40:7–8 to the purifying work of the good news and the Word of God:

John the Baptist prepared the way through baptism, forgiveness of sins, and "by blasting away at the self-righteous Pharisees and Sadducees who felt no need of a Savior."[7]

Malachi, another prophet more than a hundred years after Isaiah, said something similar: "Behold, I send my messenger, and he will prepare the way before me. And the Lord whom you seek will suddenly come to his temple; and the messenger of the covenant in whom you delight, behold, he is coming, says the LORD of hosts" (Mal. 3:1). After Malachi, the prophets were silenced for four hundred years—until John the Baptist became the messenger of Jesus.

Keep in mind that John the Baptist was not the same man as the apostle John, who wrote the gospel of John. John the Baptist, however, was a relative of Jesus (Luke 1:36).

Read Luke 1:5–14. What did the angel tell Zechariah?

What was John the Baptist called to do? (Luke 1:15–17)

Having purified your souls by your obedience to the truth for a sincere brotherly love, love one another earnestly from a pure heart, since you have been born again, not of perishable seed but of imperishable, through the living and abiding word of God; for

"All flesh is like grass
and all its glory like the flower of grass.
The grass withers,
and the flower falls,
but the word of the Lord remains forever."

And this word is the good news that was preached to you.

1 Peter 1:22–25

How did John the Baptist fulfill his calling? (Refer back to Matthew 3:1–12.)

Read Matthew 14:1–13 and Mark 6:14–29. What happened to John the Baptist?

When Jesus heard about John's death, He withdrew "to a desolate place by himself" (Matt. 14:13). Why do you think He did so? What does this tell you about Jesus?

Chapter 40 is a turning point in Isaiah's message, and here we find the key to the gospel message: the Lord will appear and all flesh will see Him—and while the things of this earth will wither and fade, the word of our God will stand forever. Jesus will stand forever.

In the "near" time, these verses were meant to encourage God's people who were going to face the destruction of Jerusalem and captivity in Babylon. They needed to remember how fleeting this world can be and stand firm on the promises of God. In the "far" time, about six hundred years later, Jesus would appear in the flesh, before thousands of Jewish people, and fulfill these words.

WHAT'S THE POINT?

In "our" time, we can use these words to encourage us. Jesus was real. People saw Him in the flesh. The promises of God still stand forever, while the pain of this world will wither and fade.

God often sends people to prepare the way for His presence. Who prepared the way for you to come to know the Lord?

How did that person prepare the way for you?

I think it's every Christian's job to prepare the way for Jesus in someone's life. We do it by example, by mentoring, by serving in children's ministry, with our neighbors, and so on.

How are you preparing the way for someone else?

HOW DO WE USE IT?

If you struggled to write how you were preparing the way for someone else to come to know Jesus, you are not alone! But, it is time to get more intentional about spreading the good news.

We don't need to go out into the desert and eat locusts like John the Baptist to tell people about Jesus. That definitely would *not* work these days! But we may have to get out of our comfort zone. What comfort do you need to leave behind and push away in order to prepare the way for Jesus? Remember that "preparing the way" does not always mean you will be the one who leads someone to Christ. You are just preparing the way.

Write just one step you could take this week to begin building the path to Jesus for someone else.[8]

Also, we can use the fact that the Word of our God will stand forever. It will not change. He will not falter or forget His promises to us. Be encouraged. Lift your chin in tough times and look to the Lord for comfort.

How could the promises of God in Isaiah 35 comfort you this week? Write some of those promises here:

I Am He

ISAIAH 41

Today, we're taking a brief departure from our normal study method. We will take a long look at Isaiah 41 and ask ourselves, "Who is God?" That's an awfully big question to answer, but I believe through Isaiah 41, God has issued a challenge to us: Who else is able to predict the future?

He asked His chosen people (and that's us now) to consider who else could do what He has done, and to consider whether they were relying on the works of their hands, that is, their false gods.

There are two sections that are prophecies in this chapter. Both are considered to be about the king of Persia, who would bring down the Babylonian Empire and eventually free the Jewish people to return to Jerusalem and rebuild the temple and their city. Later, in Isaiah 44 and 45, God will call this person by name, approximately 150 years before he (Cyrus) was born. It is one of the most specific prophecies that have been fulfilled from the Bible. But here in chapter 41, the Lord is only referencing Cyrus, without naming him. I think God is doing this now, before He names Cyrus, to force us to consider who else could predict the future. Who could?

God wants us to ponder and then answer the question correctly: no one but the one true God, Creator of all things, sovereign above all things could predict the future like He does in the Bible. Yet, I believe God goes one step further to remove any remaining doubts lingering in the backs of our minds by *naming* this man long before he is born, and certainly long before Cyrus became the king of Persia.

So, when you see "who stirred up one from the east" (v. 4), this is likely a reference to Cyrus, who approached Babylon from the east where Persia was located. Also, "I stirred up one from the north"(v. 25) likely is also referring to Cyrus because although he would approach Babylon from the east, the actual attack was from the north.[9]

Grab a highlighter and mark up Isaiah 41 in your Bible. Circle or highlight wherever God describes Himself or refers to Himself. Next, circle with a pencil wherever you think God is pointing out false gods or reliance on someone other than Him. Below, journal your thoughts as you ponder, "Who is God?"

In this chapter, God used the image of a courtroom to set up His challenge to the false gods, the idols. He calls them out to come and make an argument, to testify to the things those gods have spoken that have come to pass. Then He points out— oh yeah, they can't speak!

God points out the ridiculousness of creating something with your own hands and then worshiping it. He mocks the scene He has watched from heaven time and time again. A person grabs wood or gold to create something to represent a god, then places it somewhere on a shelf so it can be seen and worshiped. Yet, every time someone walks by or shuts a door, the darn thing tips over! So, the person gets nails and nails it down so it won't tip over at every little movement. And still the person worships this thing?! God is incensed—as well He should be.

Before we are too quick to scoff and think that's not us, consider how much time and effort you put into getting your phone, TV, or computer to work. How much do you rely on those electronics to help you deal with your life, with your circumstances, your problems, the future?

Reflect on this and write what might have become a false god—something you rely on too much—in your life:

Lately, our culture has been falling further and further into idolatry with the attitude that if I think something's true, and it's true to me, then it is truth . . . at least to me and that's good enough. The whole "you do you" thinking is founded in idolatry because it's based on the idea that we are in control of ourselves and our own lives. Nothing could be further from the truth.

Consider this: the Bible is unique in its fulfilled prophecy. No other religion can boast about specific, fulfilled prophecy like the Bible. One commentary puts it this way:

> The Bible contains the words of dozens of prophets who spoke with amazing clarity about future events—as many as two thousand specific prophecies. In Isaiah alone there are hundreds of very specific prophecies about the nations of his day. . . . By contrast, if you research Islamic prophecies, you will come up with some vague generalities, not true prophecies. Buddhism and Hinduism are not known for making any specific prophecies about world events. The bottom line is this: only the Bible has this kind of fulfilled prophecy. Isaiah 41 clearly proclaims God's stunning power to take on the idols of the world, challenging them to a simple test: declare the future, then bring it to pass.[10]

God is jealous for our reliance on Him and Him alone. He wants our gaze on Him, our heart and mind tuned in to His sovereignty. God has preserved His Word, the Bible, so that we can know that He is God, that His claims are true, and that He always does what He says He's going to do. I like how Alfred Martin put it:

> Prediction of the future is the prerogative of God alone, because He alone is the all-knowing One. This fact is often asserted in Isaiah. As has been said, prophecy is the seal that God has put on His Word to show its genuineness. It authenticates the Scripture.[11]

It does for me.

Seeing the fulfilled prophecies helps me to declare with certainty that the Bible is true. Does it for you? Why or why not?

WHAT'S THE POINT?

It's a good time to consider how you're doing. We're almost halfway through this study. Are the prophecies impacting your faith? Are you becoming more steadfast in your conviction about Jesus and the Bible? Are you *certain* the Bible is the very Word of God?

Write about it here:

How often do you consider that God is literally speaking to you through the Bible you hold in your hands? Do you pause or ponder that the words of the almighty God appear on the pages in black and white? When I was a new believer, the Holy Spirit regularly overwhelmed me as I read and studied my Bible. As I matured, the Bible became more routine to me. I began to hear God's voice more regularly and became more familiar with hearing Him speak to me through His Word. Yet,

I never want to lose my sense of awe and wonder at the power and beauty that is our Bible. If you are new to your Bible, it's okay if you are still unsure or a bit unsettled about the whole thing. We've been taught that no one can predict the future. We've been taught to be skeptical. We've been told don't believe everything you hear (or read!). It's difficult to shake off those things from our hearts and minds we were taught when we were young. As adults, logic and reasoning rule the day. If we can't make sense of something, we tend to disbelieve it. But keep challenging yourself to consider who else could do what God has done with the words you are studying.

HOW DO WE USE IT?

We use the confidence we're growing to begin changing our lives.

How does the Lord want you to rely on Him more, acknowledging His sole sovereignty with our actions or attitudes?

We can also use fulfilled prophecy to assure ourselves that our God does, in fact, speak to us. He wants to communicate with us, help us, guide us. Since Jesus came, He bestowed on His believers the incredible gift of the Holy Spirit to help us stay in constant communication with Him.

How are you listening for God to speak to you about *His* plans for *your* future?

Through Isaiah, God also told His people to "fear not!" several times. Why do you think God wants His people to set aside their fears?

What fears do you need to acknowledge and then cast from your mind into the mighty arms of your God?

Read Isaiah 41:8–14 again and write the actions God has or will take toward you:

I pray that you go through the rest of the day feeling chosen, like a friend of God. May you be strengthened and held in the righteous right hand of almighty God.

My Servant in Whom
My Soul Delights

ISAIAH 42:1–9

Isaiah 42:1–9 represents the first of the "Servant Songs" in the book of Isaiah. These Servant Songs are passages that describe the Messiah, His ministry, and His mission (also see Isa. 49:1–13; 50:4–9; and 52:13–53:12). In Isaiah 42, there are two servants referenced: the Servant of the LORD (mostly likely describing the Messiah) and "my" servant (most likely describing Israel).

The gentle descriptions of this Servant in Isaiah 42 contrast with the descriptions of other conquering kings, like Cyrus, who were described in war terms. Yet, there seems to be another blend of the first and second coming of Jesus in this passage because at first the Savior is described with gentleness, but once His praises are shouted from the ends of the earth, we see in verse 13 that

> The LORD goes out like a mighty man,
> like a man of war he stirs up his zeal;
> he cries out, he shouts aloud,
> he shows himself mighty against his foes.

Also, this Servant who would bring light to the nations and open the eyes of the blind could not be the servant nation of Israel who was described as being blind, deaf, plundered, and despoiled later in the passage. Most scholars agree this passage contains prophecy regarding the Messiah and Israel as a nation. We are going to study the part that relates to the Messiah.

Today, you will read another prophecy that was addressed in all four gospels regarding the baptism of Jesus. As you study Isaiah's words, picture the Father speaking of His Son. Ask God to give you eyes to see, ears to hear, and a heart to accept what He wants to teach you through the Scriptures today.

READ ISAIAH 42:1–9, MARKING YOUR BIBLE AS USUAL. You've already studied the account in Matthew 3:13–17 about the baptism of Jesus by John the Baptist and how God "put my Spirit upon him" (Isa. 42:1). (The baptism of Jesus is also recounted in Mark 1:9–11; Luke 3:21–22; and John 1:25–34.) Now read Matthew 17:1–6 and hear how almighty God spoke and fulfilled Isaiah's words during the transfiguration of Jesus (see also Luke 9:28–36).

Next, note how Matthew confirms Isaiah's words were written about Jesus as you read Matthew 12:15–21.

Let's go to a beautiful part of the Christmas story. Read Luke 2:25–35, and as always, feel free to mark words and phrases that pertain to the Messiah. Even though this event happened when Jesus was only eight days old, Simeon recognized Him as the "light for revelation" to the Gentiles, that is, the whole world, and thus fulfilling Isaiah 42.

In addition to the awe and wonder I experience when discovering these ancient verses fulfilled in the New Testament, I'm overwhelmed by what we learn about God and Jesus in this passage. There's so much within Isaiah 42 that I'm compelled to unpack it a bit. Bear with me and remember: He is worthy of the work!

First, consider verse 1: "Behold my servant, whom I uphold, my chosen, in whom my soul delights; I have put my Spirit upon him; he will bring forth justice to the nations."

The Father chose His Son to be the Savior of the world. The Father delights in His Son and has given Him the Spirit. God said so—out loud—at the baptism of Jesus, in front of a crowd of people lined up to be baptized that day by John the Baptist. In that same moment, with all those people present, God also sent the Spirit down to Jesus in a form that the people could see, "like a dove," so they could recognize what He had done, "put my Spirit upon him."

With regard to this baptism moment, one commentator said it this way: "With this single statement God identified Jesus as the messianic king (cf., Mt 16:16 and 26:63, where Messiah is identified as God's Son) and as His special Servant who would carry out His will and suffer to save sinners."[12]

God has never been hiding from us. God *wants* us to know Him and understand Jesus as His Son and as our Savior and Lord.

Also, the Hebrew word for "justice" used here means more than what we currently think of in legal terms. The word used for "justice" in the original Hebrew language means that the "Messiah will do all that is necessary to restore God's right order on the earth."[13]

What do you think the world will look like when "God's right order" is fully restored on earth after the second coming of Christ? What does that mean to you?

Next, reread verses 2–4 and think of what you've heard about Jesus: "He will not cry aloud or lift up his voice, or make it heard in the street; a bruised reed he will not break, and a faintly burning wick he will not quench; he will faithfully bring forth justice. He will not grow faint or be discouraged till he has established justice in the earth; and the coastlands wait for his law."

How did Jesus fulfill these words?

These words describe a Servant of God who would be humble (not promoting Himself) and deal tenderly with the hurting. If you read through the Gospels, you will see that Jesus not only failed to seek attention, but rather retreated time and time again. He often told people *not* to tell others of the miracle He just performed or who did it. As you read the account of the life of Jesus, you will hear the compassion of Christ as He walked among the sinners, the hurting, and the sick. He did not hob-nob with the celebrities of the day or seek an audience with the powerful men of His culture or government. Jesus approached the "bruised reed" and the "faintly burning wick" around Him with healing and compassion.

Has the Lord handled your hurts with compassion and gentleness?

Have you asked Him to heal you or to bind up your broken heart?

Have you allowed His lovingkindness to soften your heart and mind toward healing?

Please don't mistake the gentleness of Jesus as weakness. Remember that the Lamb is also the Lion of Judah. Jesus was resolute. He stood firm against the religious leaders because their hearts were far from God. He endured all of the abuse and rejection, faithfully firm until He restored God's justice in all the earth (vv. 3–4). In John 18 and 19, you can read how Jesus did not cry out during His trial. Silent, but resolved to fulfill His mission.

What area in your life could benefit from a faithfully firm resolution?

Next, God points out His role as Creator and Sustainer of life (again). He tells Jesus that He would hold His hand and watch over Him, appointing Him "as a covenant for the people, a light for the nations, to open the eyes that are blind, to bring out the prisoners from the dungeon, from the prison those who sit in darkness" (vv. 6–7). Jesus said He was the new covenant. He certainly healed the blind as we studied earlier this week. With His death and resurrection, Jesus freed all the earth from the dungeon or prison of sin and the darkness of death.

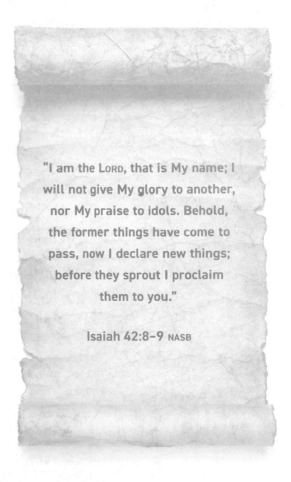

"I am the LORD, that is My name; I will not give My glory to another, nor My praise to idols. Behold, the former things have come to pass, now I declare new things; before they sprout I proclaim them to you."

Isaiah 42:8–9 NASB

The last two verses vibrate off the page for me. Read Isaiah 42:8–9 (in the margin) out loud, and put some authority in your voice.

Pause here and ask yourself this question: if Jesus *wasn't* from God, do you think God would have allowed His ministry and following to carry on the way it did, and then gain momentum into worldwide fame? Do you think if Jesus *wasn't* the Son of God, the almighty God of creation would stand for Jesus to get some of His glory?

Write your thoughts:

Also, consider verses 8–9 in light of what Jesus taught about a new covenant. At the Last Supper, Jesus said:

> And he took bread, and when he had given thanks, he broke it and gave it to them, saying, "This is my body, which is given for you. Do this in remembrance of me." And likewise the cup after they had eaten, saying, "This cup that is poured out for you is the *new covenant* in my blood." (Luke 22:19–20)

And in Mark 14:24: "And he said to them, 'This is my blood of the covenant, which is poured out for many.'" Do you see the connection with the verses from Isaiah?

Finally, we've already studied the challenge of the final phrase—who could tell us things before they happen?

Only God.

I would encourage you to read the rest of Isaiah 42 because there's more to unpack about God and Jesus. There's just not enough time in our lesson!

WHAT'S THE POINT?

Our faith in Jesus has stood the test of time. History supports our faith. We can trace our Christian heritage back to the beginning of time. Any believer in a Creator God must admit that a God who created the universe certainly could tell us what would happen and then cause it to happen. He who keeps the stars in the sky and the planets in rotation around the sun has the power to handle the events of mankind. He certainly has the power to manage my life! Can you trust Him with yours?

HOW DO WE USE IT?

Jesus gave us the example to follow. We are to be humble servants of His kingdom, pursuing what the Father would have us do each day. Be gentle. Be kind. Be on mission.

Think back on your week. Were you gentle with others, especially with the hurting? Did you promote yourself, seek attention? Write about it here:

Close your time today praying about who might need a gentle touch from you.

Review, Reflect, and Pray

Today, take some time to consider the gentleness of Jesus. Reflect on the qualities of gentleness and compassion in your own life. Write what the Holy Spirit brings to mind:

Create some sort of visual reminder to place where your not-so-gentle side most often comes out: a picture, a verse, an image of Jesus, lyrics from a song, etc.

Go back through the lessons and highlight the prophecies that had the most impact on you this week. Write the "address" of those prophecies here ("address" example: Isaiah 26:3):

Go back through the lessons and put a big question mark in the margin beside anything that you still have questions or doubts about, or where you want to learn more.

Write a prayer acknowledging Jesus as the Son and Servant of God. Thank Him for being faithful and firm to fulfill His mission to save you. Praise God that the former things have come to pass and new things are springing forth:

Week Three:
The Savior with Us

GROUP DISCUSSION OR REFLECTION QUESTIONS

1. Do you struggle to believe the miracles described in the Bible really happened? Reflect on or discuss your response to this question.

2. Why do you think God sent John the Baptist to prepare the way for Jesus? Is preparation important? How were you prepared to hear about the Lord? Who might God be preparing for you to take a step in that person's faith journey?

3. List three ideas that could pave the way to Jesus in your neighborhood or community.

4. Is your faith growing as a result of this study? Don't stop with a yes or no. Explain why you answered as you did.

5. What has surprised you so far about this study or what you've learned so far?

6. List three people who would benefit from you practicing more gentleness and compassion. What steps can you take in the lives of those you noted?

THE SAVIOR'S STRENGTH AND LOVE

This week, we'll cover a lot of territory in Isaiah. We'll see what I consider a personal love letter in Isaiah 43, the second and third Servant Songs, and a bridge to the fourth and final Servant Song. Whew. It's a lot, but so worth it! More of Jesus will be revealed to you this week. More of His mission and the glorious love of our God will be on display. We'll learn how to look backward to remember and how to look forward to sustain our hope and faith in almighty God and Jesus.

You'll never regret time spent studying His Word and trying to learn more about Him. Don't forget: He is worthy of the work!

Honored and Loved

ISAIAH 43

I wish you could see my face right now. I'm giddy. Picture me clapping my hands and squealing a bit. Why? Because we are about to study my *very* favorite chapter in the Old Testament. This chapter helped change my life. This chapter removed my lingering doubts about why God would save me by sending His Son to earth to die on a cross. This chapter defeated my desire to understand with human logic and feelings.

But wait, there's something off. This chapter has *not* been clearly identified as a messianic prophecy. Only one of the scholarly works I've been using for my research for this study includes Isaiah 43 among the prophecies pointing toward Jesus. Mostly the research points to God comforting Israel as a nation because it will face destruction and captivity before God will restore the nation.

To me, however, Jesus and His redemptive work are so clearly outlined in Isaiah 43 that it changed my life. I read Isaiah 43 as another "near" and "far" prophecy, pointing to both the upcoming events for the nation of Judah *and* the redemptive work of Jesus. Hmm . . .

I studied it again, asking whether I was including chapter 43 in this study because

I love it or because it predicts Jesus. My heart and mind stood firm that these words point to Jesus and His work on the cross. Let's see what you think!

READ AND MARK UP ISAIAH 43 IN YOUR BIBLE. Next, read John 11:49–52 and discover how Caiaphas, who was high priest, prophesied that Jesus would die for not only the nation of Israel, but also to gather the children of God scattered abroad.

As you read the passage of Isaiah 43, did you think of Jesus or the redemption He gave us through His death and resurrection? Or did you think of the Jewish people and their circumstances? Write about your thoughts, doubts, insights, or questions here:

Pastor Andrew Davis wrote:

> Some commentators on Isaiah 43 focus exclusively on the author's original intent (the author being Isaiah) and speak only about the restoration of the Jews after the exile. Yet the chapter points to a far greater achievement, that worked by Jesus Christ at the cross and by the Holy Spirit in spreading the gospel to the ends of the earth. Therefore, while we Christians should respect the historical setting for this chapter, within it we see clues that God meant to speak a word of great encouragement to every generation of his chosen people.[1]

I think either way you read Isaiah 43—as a messianic prophecy or not—you can know certain things about God from these verses that may be critical to your faith and life.

First, why Jesus would be the one and only way to heaven finally made sense to me as I read the first thirteen verses. God created me. He formed me. He controls the very breath I take. So, why would I think my salvation depended on *me* when God was in control of everything in the universe? Of course, God would do the redeeming!

READ JOHN 14:6–11. What does Jesus tell the disciples to do if they could not believe (after spending all this time with Him) that He came from the Father and that He and the Father are one?

. . . or else believe on account __ ___ _____ _____ (v. 11).

Second, He knows my name. I am His. He will be with me through the troubles on this earth. These verses make God relational: *your* God, *your* Savior. Of course, He would pay ransom for His own.

But it was this verse that stopped me in my tracks: "Since you are precious in My sight, since you are honored and *I love you*, I will give other people in your place and other nations in exchange for your life" (Isa. 43:4 NASB).

Those words all humans long to hear: *I love you*. Right there in black and white from almighty God.

God whispered lovingly into my soul as I read these verses again and again: you are rare and valuable, you hold a special place in my heart, and I love you. I love you so much I would do *anything* for you.

Almighty God, the Creator of heaven and earth, loves *you*. He loves you with such passion and desire that He would *make* a way for *you* to be with Him forever. He would figure out a way to keep His word (sin would require lifeblood), maintain His holiness and righteousness, *and* manage to get you back!

Read verses 6–7 (NASB) and hear God talking about *you*: "'I will say to the north, "Give them up!" and to the south, "Do not hold them back." Bring My sons from afar *and My daughters from the ends of the earth*, everyone who is called by My name, and whom I created for My glory, whom I have formed, even whom I have made.'"

If you're like me, the very next thought in your head is *But why? Why me? Why would God love and value me that much? I'm nothing special, but rather quite the opposite.*

Read verses 10–13 again and hear God's answer:

"You are my witnesses," declares the LORD,
"and my servant whom I have chosen,
that you may know and believe me
and understand that I am he.
Before me no god was formed,
nor shall there be any after me.
I, I am the LORD,
and besides me there is no savior.
I declared and saved and proclaimed,
when there was no strange god among you;
and you are my witnesses," declares the LORD, "and I am God.
Also henceforth I am he;
there is none who can deliver from my hand;
I work, and who can turn it back?"

It's not about you. It's about *Him*. *He* has revealed and saved and proclaimed. *Him*. No one could stand before Him or be delivered without *Him*. No savior apart from *Him*.

He formed me for *His* glory. I am His witness. He revealed and saved and proclaimed Jesus to me so that I would know that "I am He." So that I could declare He alone is God. So that my heart would be at peace when it realizes it's only *Him* who can save me, when I finally realize it's about *Him*, not me.

Have you been striving to save yourself? Have you been hoping to find an answer to that nagging longing in your soul apart from *Him*? Journal your thoughts:

Verses 18–21 point to Jesus for me because they speak of a new thing, which reminds us of the new covenant established by Jesus. This passage has Exodus-like language, but hear the urging to think forward, to let go of the past.

The last verse in our passage today, Isaiah 43:25, put the final nail on my doubting heart with regard to why Jesus is the only way to salvation and a relationship with God: "I, I am he who blots out your transgressions *for my own sake*, and I will not remember your sins."

You see, I was having trouble accepting Jesus as the *only* way to heaven. I think the problem is that well-meaning folks quote John 3:16 ("For God so loved the world") and try to convey how much God loves us. That's great. It is. But when you don't know anything else about God, it doesn't make any sense.

If God loves us so much, why is this world such a mess? If God loves me so much, why would He exclude me from paradise? If God loves me so much, why doesn't He just "beam me up"?

You get the idea? We need to beware of using love only to explain the cross or the forgiveness of sins. Jesus and the cross were all about atonement, about paying the price for the stated consequences of sin. God's love, of course, is what prompted the atonement; but speaking about love apart from atonement doesn't make sense to a pre-believer who has little knowledge of God's majesty, holiness, justice, and absolute unwillingness to share His glory with anyone or anything else. Atonement, not love, cleanses us from our sins so that we can be reunited with God.

That's what verse 25 did for me. It explained why *Jesus* is the answer, and why Jesus must have been not only *from* God but also *of* God. Go ahead, read it again: "I, I am he who blots out your transgressions for my own sake, and I will not remember your sins."

It's not about you. It's not about me. It's about *Him*. *He* will atone for your sins for *His own sake*. *He* will forgive our sins. *Him*.

As we've said, this God—the One who demands to be known as *the only* God, the One who dares any others to challenge His abilities, His creation—would never share His glory with a human. Period. God would not share His glory with you (as if you could earn your way to heaven with good works), and He wouldn't share it with Jesus, if Jesus were only a prophet or just a dynamic teacher.

If Jesus wasn't God, *God* would have told us so. Hear His voice in this passage: *I* am He. There is no other. *I* will save you ***for my own sake***. It's all about *Him*.

I finally got it. I could feel the love of almighty God for me and yet understand my need for Jesus. Ah Isaiah 43, you have my heart!

WHAT'S THE POINT?

The answers to every pre-believer question can be answered by pointing somewhere in your Bible. Here, in Isaiah 43, we can proclaim that God created us to be in a relationship with Him. He called us by name, and declared, "You are Mine!" God told us, with no disclaimers or conditions, "You are precious in My sight . . . and I love you." He told us how much we mean to Him. He told us that He would do something new and forgive our sins. *He* would do it.

He did do it! Jesus is the fulfillment of these promises and a demonstration of His righteousness and love. Jesus is the only way because God would never share His glory.

HOW DO WE USE IT?

We start becoming more intentional in our own relationships. First, we make sure our relationship with God is solid. Improving our relationship with Him seems to be His motivation toward us throughout the Bible. Perhaps it's time for us to start putting our relationship with *Him* at the center of our motivation.

Is your relationship with God at the very center of your life? Circle one:

Yes   Mostly   Maybe   Kind of   No

Would you like Him to be? Do you really want God to be the central purpose of your life? Write your thoughts:

That's a really difficult question, isn't it? If I don't answer a resounding and enthusiastic "yes!" I feel like a "bad" Christian. What if my answer is lukewarm? What if I don't know?

Friends, these are good questions to ponder and pray about. I think there are seasons and reasons we might shift in and out of enthusiasm to pursue our relationship with God in that wholehearted, passionate way. I think it's normal. I don't have to like it, but I do think it happens to all of us, even the most devoted. But it is always good to check on the status, health, and passion of our walk with the Lord. It's not until we notice our distance from God that we can turn back into His arms. Remember, *He* never moves, *we* do . . . and He patiently and graciously awaits our return. Isaiah 43 even helps me believe that He *longs* for our intimacy as much as I do.

Next, we make sure our relationships in our family are as loving and firm as our God loves us. We call them by name . . . *lovingly*. We tell them, "You are mine!" We tell them they are precious and honored by us. We tell them we love them.

Finally, we put relationships at the front of our efforts to spread the gospel. The good news, after all, is about relationships—with God and one another. Build those acquaintances into friendships. Build those friendships into sisterhoods! Inside those relationships God will reveal and proclaim who *He* is.

Write the name of one acquaintance you could try to focus into a friendship:

Take a few moments to pray for the person whose name you wrote down.

WEEK 4 | DAY 2

Servant of the Lord

ISAIAH 49:1–13

Short detour! Before we skip ahead to Isaiah 48 and 49, I don't want you to miss Isaiah 44:24–45:13. Grab just a few extra minutes today and see how God named a man, Cyrus, who would free the Jewish people from captivity in Babylon and send them home to Jerusalem to rebuild the city and temple. Isaiah wrote these things about someone named Cyrus long before the man was born and long before Persia would become a power bold enough to defeat Babylon. Yet, check out how specific this prophecy is in Isaiah 44:24–45:13. Cyrus is named. First of all, that's astonishing. There's no wiggle room for interpretation here. Cyrus would do it. Cyrus did it! Oh, you simply must read it.

Seriously, it's not a messianic prophecy, but it's totally worth your time and sense of awe!

I'll wrap up our short detour with what Isaiah 45:13 says about Cyrus: "'I have stirred him in righteousness, and I will make all his ways level; he shall build my city and set my exiles free, not for price or reward,' says the LORD of hosts."

And Cyrus did just that. Cyrus issued a decree that the Jewish people could return home and rebuild the temple (see 2 Chron. 36:22–23). Cyrus even let the people bring back the silver, gold, and other articles stolen from the temple (i.e., "not for price or reward")! See Ezra 1:1–11; 5:13–17; and 6:1–5 for more about this interesting turn of events.

Okay, we're back on the highway of messianic prophecies—let's get to work! Today, you'll study the second Servant Song in Isaiah.

READ AND MARK UP ISAIAH 49:1–13 IN YOUR BIBLE. Let's remember what Simeon said when he met baby Jesus at the temple. Read Luke 2:27–32 in the margin. Underline "salvation" and circle "a light for revelation to the Gentiles."

You may know that the Jewish people had been awaiting their Messiah for hundreds of years. What we might not realize today is how groundbreaking an idea it was that the Jewish Messiah was also to be available to non-Jews, that is, to Gentiles.

Read Acts 13:44–47. Why had the apostles begun to preach the gospel to the Gentiles? (v. 47)

> And he came in the Spirit into the temple, and when the parents brought in the child Jesus, to do for him according to the custom of the Law, he took him up in his arms and blessed God and said,
>
> "Lord, now you are letting your servant depart in peace, according to your word;
> for my eyes have seen your salvation that you have prepared in the presence of all peoples,
> a light for revelation to the Gentiles, and for glory to your people Israel."
>
> Luke 2:27–32

Something that can trip people up as they read Isaiah is trying to figure out who is talking! Is it Isaiah, God, or Jesus? I would encourage you to remember that these were spoken messages first, and often in poetry. So, relax a bit. To me, the most important thing is to hear the message. What is God saying through these words? Who pops into your mind as you read the words? To me, allowing the Holy Spirit to use these words to speak to me is the most important part of Bible study.

Yes, we want to keep the author, audience, historical, and cultural things in mind as we try to figure out what the text means. But don't forget that the Word of God is living and active, capable of reaching your heart and your mind, if you let it.

You can also get turned around in Isaiah by the use of Israel, Judah, Jacob, Zion. In this passage, there is some controversy over whether the use of "Israel" means that Isaiah 49:1–13 is about the nation as God's servant, not Jesus. Yet, the servant is going to bring Israel back to God. Many commentators assert that "my servant, Israel" in verse 3 is referencing Jesus, and that Jesus will be the perfect "Israel" (God's chosen; a light for God) because the nation failed at their assignment and covenant with God.

I suggest you grab two different color highlighters. Now, read Isaiah 49:1–13 again and highlight in one color when you think God the Father is speaking to or about the Son and the work the Son will do. Use the other color when you think Jesus, the Son, is speaking.

Do you get frustrated or bogged down sometimes when you study your Bible?

Guess what? Me too! And so do the scholars. This isn't easy, my friend. Press on!

One of my favorite lines in today's passage is verse 6 when the Father says to Jesus, "It is too light a thing that you should be my servant to raise up the tribes of Jacob and to bring back the preserved of Israel; I will make you a light for the nations, that my salvation may reach to the end of the earth."

Saving the Jewish people was and still is the work of the Messiah, but God loves and honors His Son so much that *all* the people, *all* the nations, *to the ends of the earth*, have the opportunity to find their salvation in Jesus!

I'd like you to notice something about this passage that's also true of Isaiah 43, and really throughout the book of Isaiah: God's grace would simply be handed down from heaven. He will pour out grace and forgiveness *for His own sake*, not because of anything we do.

Have you spent any time pondering why God would give you the chance to accept the atonement of Jesus for the forgiveness of your sins? Journal your thoughts:

Through the Old Testament, there is a pattern with the Jewish people. They would be obedient to God for a while and enjoy the blessings of walking in the will of God. But they could never keep it up. Eventually, they always fell away from God, started worshiping the gods of the foreign nations around them, and suffered God's consequences as a result.

Reading Israel's history might give you an idea that God only blesses when He is obeyed. That's what I thought my whole childhood and well into my adult years. I thought God set out a super-high standard and I had no chance of meeting it. I was doomed, I figured, so why bother with God at all.

It wasn't until I had my encounter with God in the moments when my son was dying that I turned my heart and mind back toward God. I got a tiny glimpse of heaven in a momentary feeling that washed over me like a tidal wave—and receded again like a passing shadow. But I felt it. It was real and beyond comprehension in beauty and pleasure.[2]

At that point, I knew only two things: heaven was real and I wanted to go there.

I began my Christian faith with the mindset that I would do what it took to go to heaven. If there was a super-high standard, I'd have to figure out a way to meet it.

Soon I learned that nothing could be further from the truth. Being able to earn your relationship with God, even earning your way into heaven is a complete lie. The only thing that gets you into heaven is God's grace. Accept His free love-offering in the sacrifice of Jesus—or not. If you accept His gift of eternal life you are saved to be with Him forever. If you reject Him, you will not be in heaven. It's as clear-cut as that.

It wasn't until I pored over the words of Isaiah that God's voice finally got through my preconceived and incorrect notions about Him. Through Isaiah, I finally got a glimpse of *God*, the Holy One of Israel.

Have you ever had a glimpse of God? Write about it here:

If you've not truly found God or have never felt His presence before, I'd encourage you to slow down through this study. Perhaps read every chapter in Isaiah looking specifically for your God, your Redeemer, your Savior. He is worthy of the work!

Throughout Isaiah 40–66, God was letting us know that *He* would fix the situation, *for His own sake*. John Oswalt said it this way:

> Note that Sinai [where Moses received the ten commandments] does not precede the Exodus. This fact indicates that the descendants of Jacob were not saved from Egypt by their obedience. They were delivered from that bondage by grace alone. Then, *and only then*, came the call for obedience. Obedience never produces deliverance, but gracious deliverance should issue in obedience.

> That is the paradigm presented here in Isaiah. To be sure, God calls his people to listen to and believe the promises he makes to deliver them. But his grace is declared to them even before they are necessarily prepared to listen and believe. Nor is the grace presented in any way that makes it conditional on obedience. God simply announces through the prophet that he *will* deliver them. It is stated as fact (emphasis in original).[3]

Before today, had you ever noticed that God rescued His people before He expected obedience from them? This was a huge revelation for me.

Have you long known and understood about this grace? Or have you been striving to be "good enough" for God? Write about it here:

Next, write a prayer thanking God for His grace alone. Don't start thanking Him for your blessings! Those have nothing to do with His grace toward you. Write about His grace gift:

WHAT'S THE POINT?

I don't want you to miss two more things from today's passage in Isaiah 49. First, did you notice that Jesus said He was formed and named in His mother's womb and given the tools to accomplish the mission (vv. 1–3)? We too are formed and named in our mother's womb for a mission. We too have been given the tools to accomplish our own missions!

Second, Jesus will feel like He toiled in vain, spent His strength for nothing and vanity. For these feelings, He will turn to God the Father and seek His reward with God (v. 4). In addition, the Father Himself noted that Jesus will be the "one deeply despised" and the One "abhorred by the nation," but God reassured Jesus that kings and princes will bow before Him (v. 7).

Sister, if Jesus felt like He toiled in vain, it's a sure thing that we will feel the same way! I think we have a skewed view of Jesus if we picture Him as always positive, calm, and content. He did have feelings. He did get frustrated, even angry. If He was despised and rejected, it stands to reason that we will also face such things. Yet don't forget that Jesus sought His reward and His glory from God as He faithfully fulfilled His mission.

What's your mission? What have you been called and equipped to do? Are you faithfully fulfilling your mission?

What are you frustrated with? What are you discouraged about? Write those things and take them to God. Seek His face for your "reward."

At the end, after describing the mission of Jesus (vv. 8–12), praise was the natural result in verse 13:

> Sing for joy, O heavens, and exult, O earth;
> break forth, O mountains, into singing!
> For the Lord has comforted his people
> and will have compassion on his afflicted.

God is rejoicing over all your efforts to serve His kingdom too. Bask in it!

HOW DO WE USE IT?

Keep your eyes and heart focused on the actions and character of your God as you study your Bible. Notice how your soul is stirred up by what you are reading. Allow the Holy Spirit to do His great work in you through these ancient words.

Write just ONE next step you could take to fulfill your mission:

WEEK 4 | DAY 3

Focused on the Mission

ISAIAH 50:1–11

Today, we study the third Servant Song, Isaiah 50:4–11. The heart and mission of Jesus are gaining specificity in this song. The four songs seem to build in detail and intensity. In this Servant Song, "Jehovah Adonai" is used four times, but nowhere else in the Servant Songs. The use of "Lord GOD" or "Jehovah Adonai" can be translated as "Sovereign LORD" and the emphasis is on the Servant's submission to the will of the Sovereign Lord, God the Father.[4]

READ AND MARK UP ISAIAH 50:1–11 IN YOUR BIBLE.

The first three verses are God speaking to the chosen people of Judah. He is reminding them that their upcoming exile into Babylon was the result of their sin. Judah's difficult times were not the result of God sending the people away, but rather God's people choosing sin and disobedience—distance from God—that would cause their destruction and exile.

While we know that difficult times are not always the result or consequences of sin, we do know that sometimes God allows the natural consequences of our sins to invade and destroy our lives. It's true. We don't like to say it out loud, but we must. Sometimes, the junk in my life is my own fault. There's no one to blame but myself.

Can you recall a time when your sin created a terrible situation? Can you write about it yet? If so, do it here:

If you're not ready to write about it, at least whisper it out loud to yourself. Your acknowledgment may be all you need to have a breakthrough toward healing. If you can't think of a time when your sin brought about painful consequences, I'd like to meet you! And, I have to be bold with you here, you should reexamine yourself and look again. Be honest before God. Ask Him to show you so you can grow more like Jesus each day.

God reminded His people, and us today, that He is powerful to deliver us from whatever our circumstances might be. I love that He said, "Is my hand shortened, that it cannot redeem? Or have I no power to deliver?" (v. 2).

What problems are you facing that you feel powerless to change? What problems have you discouraged?

Next, write in a different color "God has the power to change this!" over the top of what you wrote. Say it out loud. If you've confessed and repented of any sin on your part, start claiming *His* power over your problems. Or do you think God is powerless to help you? Or have you (or others) convinced yourself that He *won't* fix it? Journal your thoughts and prayers here:

Starting in verse 4, the words are considered to be spoken by the Servant of the Lord, Jesus Christ. I can't wait until I actually hear the voice of Jesus in heaven, but I love it when I can hear a bit of His personality come out when I read His Word. I also love it when my Savior sets Himself apart from the things of this world and other gods people worship.

Have you ever heard of another religion whose god is both so humble and yet so victorious? Have you heard of another one stepping down from His throne to put Himself at the mercy of the very people He created, only to be mocked, beaten, rejected, spat upon, and killed? Who else? What else? Anything? Anyone?

None. There is no other. Only God. Only Jesus.

Read John 8:28–29. How does Jesus explain His obedience to the Father?

When you think of the ministry of Jesus, what scenes come to mind? Which stories from the Gospels stick in your heart about Jesus? List a few here:

I think verse 4 gives us insight about how Jesus did those things while He was here on earth. Isn't it just like Jesus to give the Father the glory? Jesus tells us in Isaiah 50:4 that "the Lord God" gave Him the ability to disciple and to speak words that would sustain the weak and weary. How often did Jesus tell the weary to come to Him? Yet, here, does He take the credit? No, He points us to the Father.

While Jesus was here, He told us plainly, "My teaching is not mine, but his who sent me" (John 7:16) and "For I have not spoken on my own authority, but the

Father who sent me has himself given me a commandment—what to say and what to speak" (John 12:49).

We also know that Jesus withdrew early in the morning, by Himself, to pray (see Mark 1:35). In verse 4 of Isaiah 50, the Servant is telling us God awakens me morning by morning; He awakens my ear to listen as a disciple.

I think God is always waiting for us to wake up early and listen as a student, eager to learn from Him. Do you make time each day to listen to God? What time of the day do you listen to God?

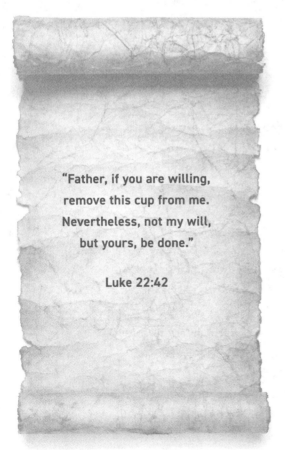

"Father, if you are willing, remove this cup from me. Nevertheless, not my will, but yours, be done."

Luke 22:42

As much as I love Bible studies, I would suggest adding a time where you simply arise and listen for what God would say to you each day, morning by morning. It's a beautiful thing to do.

Note the Servant of the Lord would not turn back from what He would have to endure (Isa. 50:5–6). Next, see the determination of Jesus to follow the will of our Father. He would be obedient, not turning back, even from the judgment of sin and death on the cross. Read Luke 22:42 in the margin and think about what Jesus prayed in the garden just before His arrest and crucifixion.

Is there anything or anyone you would give your life for? Who would you endure hours of torture for? It's a high cost, isn't it? There would have to be a lot of love to feed such fierce determination.

Do you think of God and Jesus as loving you with a fierce determination? Why or why not?

I love the phrase "I have set my face like flint" in Isaiah 50:7. Read John 18 and 19 and see if you can picture the face of Jesus set like flint.

Why do you think Jesus was so determined?

WHAT'S THE POINT?

I think part of what made Jesus so determined is contained in Isaiah 50:8–9:

> He who vindicates me is near.
> Who will contend with me?
> Let us stand up together.
> Who is my adversary?
> Let him come near to me.
> Behold, the Lord God helps me;
> who will declare me guilty?

Jesus knew the victory was at hand. He was fighting to get us back. He knew that our Father in heaven is the most mighty and awesome God, Creator of all things under heaven and on earth.

I think the point of this passage, this insight into our Savior, is really an example for us to follow. Keep your face set like flint. Be determined to follow the will of our Father in heaven.

Jesus told the disciples, "I will no longer talk much with you, for the ruler of this world is coming. He has no claim on me, but I do as the Father has commanded me, so that the world may know that I love the Father" (John 14:30–31).

If you're facing a step of obedience that is terrifying or very difficult, remember that the Father stands ready to vindicate us in the face of our enemies. Who can declare you guilty if the Lord God helps you? Be not afraid. Do not let your heart be troubled. Jesus has overcome the world (John 16:33).

HOW DO WE USE IT?

We take that next step. We set our determination. We face our enemies. We give our backs, our cheeks, our face, our heart, our very lives to do the will of God. Wow, that's a tall order isn't it? I can hardly bear it as I type it! Yet, it is what I hear from the Father as I study and write this lesson. He is calling us to be determined, in the face of our enemies, to obey Him and His Word.

What is the Lord asking you to become determined about? Where do you need to take a stand, resolute in your determination to follow the Word of God or the will of God?

For each of us, that will look different. What the Lord asks of me, He may not ask of you. What God requires of me, He may not require of you. Be careful not to judge someone else's obedience. You have no idea what the Lord is speaking into her ear.

We follow Isaiah 50:10 and obey the Servant of the Lord and "trust in the name of the LORD and rely on his God."

WEEK 4 | DAY 4

Looking Backward
to Hope Forward

ISAIAH 51

Today's prophecy is less about Jesus and more about the Father, our Creator, and His sovereign control of our world. We humans need constant reminders that this earth and our lives are only *temporary*. The troubles we face each day, the state of the world and culture we live in, all seek to bring us down, encouraging us to dwell in darkness or seek worldly pleasures to avoid our impatience for heaven. I believe Isaiah 51 sounds like the drumbeat of our Father's heart: look to Him and Him alone for our comfort, our security, keeping our focus on Him. He wants us to listen to Him, remember all that He has already done for us, and keep our eyes on what's truly important—Him and eternity in His new heaven and earth.

Isaiah 51 is a bridge between the third and fourth Servant Songs. I believe this chapter is here to call out to our broken hearts, encourage us to find our faith by looking both backward (to what's already been done) and forward (to what will come), and reset our focus on eternity. The prophecies in this chapter relate to what will happen in the future, often referred to as the "end times."

Although we're studying those prophecies about Jesus, sometimes it's important to

WEEK 4: THE SAVIOR'S STRENGTH AND LOVE   135

look into our future with hopeful expectation. If God fulfilled all the prophecies we've been studying about Christ, surely He will fulfill the prophecies, like these in Isaiah 51, regarding the return of Christ and eternity. In chapter 51, God is both reminding the Israelites what He had already done for them and what He would do in their future (with regard to freeing them from both Babylonian captivity *and* eventually from this temporary world).

I want you to read all of chapter 51 because I think there are different parts that will resonate with each person. Each of us can see ourselves and our lives in different portions of this Scripture.

As you ponder today's verses, take time to remember what God has already done in your own life. Enjoy this bit of encouragement about your future from your heavenly Father. A glorious future awaits!

READ ISAIAH 51 IN YOUR BIBLE and, as we have been doing, feel free to mark up the passage.

Study what Jesus told us about the "end times" in Matthew 24:34–39. Next, read Peter's teaching in 2 Peter 3:1–13 about keeping what the prophets have told us in our minds.

One thing that comes loud and clear to me from Isaiah 51 is frustration. God wants to know why we continue to fear what people can do to us and ignore what *He* can do for us. Why do we focus so much on our troubles rather than turning to the God of the universe? God seems to be asking us why we can't remember who He is and what He's capable of.

Why do we tremble, anxious about what is happening to us, when that trouble is only temporary? Journal your thoughts:

If you have children, you know how all those baby shots can be anxiety-producing. How will your little one deal with the pain he can't understand? We used to tell our boys, even when they were very little, that a shot only hurts for less than ten seconds. By the time we count to ten, it won't hurt anymore. Just before the shot, we would tell them to look at our eyes and count with us to ten.

That's how I feel about Isaiah 51. God is telling us to look at Him, listen to Him, remember His power—and count to ten—because eventually a new heaven and new earth will be created for His people. If we can just keep our eyes on God, and remind ourselves that this pain is only temporary, we can make it through the troubles of this world.

A grieving mom grieves every single day. Every. Single. Day. This life sure feels long. I know that life can feel very hard and very long. But never forget what God's Word tells us. Read 2 Peter 3:8–9 in the margin.

Fill in these blanks: The Lord is _____ _____ to fulfill his promise. He is _____ toward me.

Read Revelation 21:3–6 and consider putting it on an index card to keep near at hand (like I do sometimes) for encourgagement. God will keep His promise to fix this broken world. He will. He said so.

What encouragement did you get from the verses we studied today?

> **But do not overlook this one fact, beloved, that with the Lord one day is as a thousand years, and a thousand years as one day. The Lord is not slow to fulfill his promise as some count slowness, but is patient toward you, not wishing that any should perish, but that all should reach repentance.**
>
> **2 Peter 3:8–9**

I think the length of time is what causes us to focus on the present. Life feels long. It sure lasts longer than the ten seconds we counted with our boys! If only we knew *when* God would send Christ back and create that new heaven and earth, then we might be able to withstand our hardships with more hope.

But, sister, that's what the Word of God is for: to stand in the gap when we don't remember and to comfort us when we lose hope. It's the main purpose of this study. To remind you that God told us He would send Jesus so that you can become steadfast in your faith. We study the Word to be reminded, to gain knowledge, to be comforted, to draw near to God, to increase our hope.

Write about two times in your life when something went "right" for you:

Looking back, can you see God's hand in those circumstances? Write about it:

I think it's natural for many of us to focus on the negative things in this world. Yet, God has done more *for* us than He has allowed against us!

Write one verse from the passages you studied today that can shift your focus to God or eternity:

What parts of God's character do you think show up most in Isaiah 51?

What areas of your life could benefit from more trust in the God who always keeps His promises?

One commentary said this of Isaiah 51: "God wants them to listen to him! He desires to feed their faith by his words."[5]

Oh how I want you to see that is true! Do you see how God wants to feed your faith through His words? Why else would He have told us before it happened, had it recorded on scrolls, and protected the Bible to remain all this time?

God wants you to be encouraged by His Word. When discouragement rises, return to listen to Him. When fears surround you, shift your focus to the Ancient of Days and remember His works. When life feels long, imagine when Christ will split the sky and this earth will fade away.

WHAT'S THE POINT?

Our focus. If we're looking backward into the past, it should be to remember God's faithfulness, His power, His sovereignty. Not to rehash our mistakes, sit in self-sabotaging memories, or wallow in self-pity. If we are fearing things in this world, or feeling deep pain or despair, we can shift our focus to Him and our eternal life that is to come.

Our hope. It is a hope filled with expectation. We can look forward to an end of the pain of this world. God has promised that He will make all things new.

Can you identify three things you look forward to in heaven?

HOW DO WE USE IT?

I love this quote: "The future should empower the present as much as the past does."[6] It's so true. We can use the requests and assurances in Isaiah 51 to empower us to live in joyous expectation. When great things are happening, it's easy to be joyful and filled with peace. It's when life gets hard and long that our joyful expectation seems to fade. Yet, if we're *certain* a beautiful and perfect life awaits us, then how long should we despair? How long should we allow this world to keep us down?

Fight back, my friend! Use the future to empower your attitude and shift your focus to heaven and our eternal, all-powerful God. Glory awaits every believer, not a few lucky winners. Every. Single. Believer. Grab hold of your future and don't let go!

Review, Reflect, and Pray

Use this list as a timeline and record a few *good* things that happened to you in each stage:

Pre-Kindergarten (ages 0–5):

Elementary School (ages 5–14):

High School (ages 15–18):

Post-High School or College (ages 19–22):

Early Adulthood (ages 22–32):

Adulthood (ages 33–53):

Later Adulthood (ages 54–64):

Golden Years (ages 65 and up):

Write a prayer of thanks for all these good things in your past:

Go back through the lessons and highlight the prophecies that had the most impact on you this week. Write the "address" of those prophecies here ("address" example: Isaiah 26:3):

Go back through the lessons and put a big question mark in the margin beside anything that you still have questions or doubts about, or where you want to learn more.

Write a prayer to God to help you let go of any "not so good" moments in your life because you are shifting your focus to your future—a future that is certain to be glorious and perfect:

Week Four:
The Savior's
Strength and Love

GROUP DISCUSSION OR REFLECTION QUESTIONS

1. Do you struggle to remember the good things that happened to you? If so, why do you think you have this tendency?

2. With all the negative news and tragedies in this life, how will you keep focused on our good and gracious God? What verses from this week's lessons or elsewhere in the Bible can help you focus?

3. Why should we spend time thinking about heaven and eternity?

4. When is it helpful to remember the past? When should we not dwell on what is past? List three ideas that could help you shift your focus away from the past and into the glorious future of eternity with God.

5. Is your faith floundering or focused right now? Would your answer be different from what you would have said a month ago?

6. What ways should the love of God change your attitude each day?

7. Think about how God asked His people to look/pay attention, listen to Him, and awaken in Isaiah 51. How is God calling you to do these things today?

THE SAVIOR'S SACRIFICE

About the topic of our study this week, Dr. Warren Wiersbe, quoting Old Testament scholar Dr. Kyle Yates, called the passage of our study this week "the Mount Everest of messianic prophecy."[1] We will be studying the fourth Servant Song, often called the Suffering Servant. Isaiah 52:13–15 and all of Isaiah 53 forecast the trial and crucifixion of Jesus.

For me, this week's passage is actually the "easiest" to confirm of all the messianic prophecies in Isaiah. In my opinion, the mind-blowing details contained in Isaiah 52:13–53:12 are clear and convincing proof that Jesus is, without a doubt, the Messiah. There is no other way all of those details could line up with anyone other than Jesus Christ. Further, in Luke 22:37, just before His arrest, Jesus told the disciples directly that Isaiah 53:12, "and he was numbered with transgressors," had its fulfillment in Him.

Of course, orthodox Jews deny the messianic nature of Isaiah 52:13–53:12. Prevailing Jewish teachings put Israel as a nation in the place of the Suffering Servant, submitting that the nation of Israel must suffer so that the nations of the world might be saved through its sacrificial suffering. Such an interpretation, however, ignores at least three basic facts:

(1) Isaiah consistently described the nation of Israel as the sinner, rebellious and forsaking God, while the servant in this passage is without guilt and righteous;

(2) the pronoun used refers most often to an individual in ancient Hebrew; and

(3) the details in these verses match the atoning work of Christ, His crucifixion, and His glorious exaltation too closely to be anything other than prophetic Scripture about Jesus Christ.[2]

Interestingly, the portion of the Dead Sea Scrolls that contains Isaiah includes all sixty-six chapters of this book. Experts estimate that the scroll was written around a hundred years before Christ![3] Based on Isaiah's description of the Jewish leaders and the history of Israel and Judah, we know that Isaiah spoke these prophecies at least six hundred years before Jesus was born. The age testing conducted on the Dead Sea Scrolls is an objective confirmation that the words of Isaiah were written hundreds of years before Jesus was born.

If you've never read Isaiah 52–53 before, buckle up for one amazing week! If you've studied these passages before, I pray a deeper revelation settles over your soul this week. I pray for the Holy Spirit to bring to your mind all the teachings of Jesus as you read the ancient words of Isaiah. While I think this week's passage is the easiest to declare a messianic prophecy that was fulfilled by Jesus Christ, it is also one of the most difficult passages in Scripture to pore over, study, and reflect upon. The death of Jesus was no easy thing. I'll be praying over you as you tackle the tough parts of this week's study. Remember, He is worthy of the work!

Unexplainable Servant

ISAIAH 52:13–15

These first few verses of the Suffering Servant we'll study today are a sharp contrast to one another. The Servant shall be highly exalted, lifted up, astonishing—yet, His appearance will be so bad that He no longer appears human—but, kings will be speechless when they understand the Servant. How strange!

Let's see if we can sort this out.

Read Isaiah 52:13–15. As always, feel free to mark up your Bible. Below, journal how you think each verse may relate to Jesus:

Next, read Romans 15:17–21 and summarize why Paul thought his ministry was part of the fulfillment of Isaiah 52:15:

Isaiah had used the same phrase, "shall be high and lifted up," in reference to God Himself (see Isa. 6:1).[4] It does not seem likely that the prophet Isaiah would use the same words to describe the nation of Israel, especially not during the prophet's time. It also doesn't make sense that Isaiah would use these same words to describe another human being. The servant referenced here must be something special.

Read John 17:1–5 and summarize what Jesus is asking that fulfills Isaiah 52:13:

The scourging (whipping) of Jesus would have left Him beyond recognition and nearly dead. Read Matthew 27:26–31 and summarize what happened to Jesus:

The Roman scourge whip was a short leather whip with several "tails" that had pieces of bone and metal designed to tear the skin, sometimes to the bone. Because the scourge was so deadly, the Jewish people limited it to forty lashes. The Romans, however, had no such rule. The Jews turned Jesus over to the Romans because they were not permitted to put anyone to death and they wanted Jesus dead. Even though the Jewish leaders knew what the Roman scourging could do to a man, they wanted more. Pilate told them he would punish (scourge) Jesus, but it wasn't enough.

READ LUKE 23:13–24.

How many times did Pilate say, "I will therefore punish and release him"?

———

Jesus, the Son of God, was beaten, spat upon, scourged, tortured with a crown of thorns, all *before* He was crucified. Before they lifted His cross up into position, Jesus likely would have been "so marred, beyond human semblance, and his form beyond that of the children of mankind" (Isa. 52:14).

We should sit here a moment. Let's not rush over the horrific details. We should take a long hard look at our Savior.

We should not lose sight of the torture Jesus went through so that verse 15 could be possible ("so shall he sprinkle many nations").

Write a prayer thanking Him for being willing to leave His glory to rescue you, to become your substitute, to experience all the pain of that day, to atone for your sins:

Some translators chose "startle" or "cleanse," rather than "sprinkle." In the context of the other verses surrounding the word, I agree it should be translated as "sprinkle" because the same word is used in Leviticus 4 and 16, and in Numbers 19, when blood is to be sprinkled on the altar or to "clean" the temple or the priests.

WHAT'S THE POINT?

The Suffering Servant, Jesus, the highly exalted Son of God, would endure terrible pain in order to "sprinkle" the nations with His atoning blood. Kings (implying His scope would be far reaching and powerful) would be speechless when they understood what happened to Jesus and why He did it. Kings, the most powerful people on the planet, would see a lesson in humility, love, sacrifice, justice, mercy, and holiness.

When you think of what God endured to provide Jesus as your substitute, doesn't it make you speechless too? Write what you felt when you first realized what Jesus did for you. Add what you feel today as you reflect on His sacrifice:

HOW DO WE USE IT?

We don't rush past the ugliness of the cross to get to the good stuff of our forgiveness. We take time throughout the year to stop and reflect on the death of Jesus.

When I teach on the topic of atonement, I wear a prison orange jumpsuit—signifying that *all* of us should be wearing prison orange every single day of our lives. Without Jesus, we were *all* on death row. Each and every sin, no matter how big or small, carries the penalty of death. There is no city court for parking tickets, or misdemeanor court for minor offenses, in front of the judgment seat of God. Lifeblood is required for *any* sin.

When Jesus stepped off His throne in heaven, He came down to this earth, He walked up to you and removed your prison orange jumpsuit—set you free from death row—placed that orange jumpsuit on *Himself*, and walked straight into the death chamber in your place.

At this point, I usually yell just a little bit, "IT WAS ***NOT*** A PARDON!"

A pardon means your sentence is over and you get out of jail. A pardon means you go free. A pardon means you get to go on living, outside of jail. God did not issue a pardon to you. Your sins are not forgiven because God loves you and decided to save you or set you free.

"SOMEONE DIED!" I'm usually still shouting a bit. "Someone took your orange jumpsuit, walked down death row, was strapped down on a cold medical table, and took a needle in the arm, and DIED!"

Often I'm overcome with emotion as I next whisper, "It. Was. Not. A. Pardon. *Jesus*, the only Son of God, died with *my* ugly orange prison jumpsuit draped over His holy and righteous body. *Jesus* took *my* death penalty injection into *His* arm and died in my place. He died. Actually, Jesus died much more horribly than today's death chamber. In my place."

Even more stunning: He set me free to sit in heaven with His Father, in *His* place, to share *His* inheritance (see John 17; Eph. 2:6; Rev. 3:21). It's inconceivable.

We can use the death of Christ and these shocking words of Isaiah to remain in awe of what Jesus did for us. We never take it for granted.

We tell people about it—this amazing Savior and God—who was willing to take our place and die so that our sins could be forgiven by the Holy One of Israel.

Have you been thinking of the forgiveness of your sins as a pardon? Explain.

How will remembering that *Jesus* paid the penalty for *your* sins change your daily walk with the Lord?

WEEK 5 | DAY 2

Suffering Servant

ISAIAH 53:1–3

Today, we'll study the unlikely aspects of Jesus and His ministry. We'll look on as the King of kings, the Lord of lords, the Prince of Peace, and Wonderful Coun- selor is despised and rejected. Remember, this is "the Mount Everest of messianic prophecy" . . . so it isn't going to be easy! You can do it. A friend of mine had a sign in her office that said, "We can do hard things." That's how I feel about the fourth Servant Song. We can study hard things.

MARK UP ISAIAH 53:1–3 IN YOUR BIBLE. Next, read another amazing declaration from Jesus that the Scriptures would be fulfilled through Him in Luke 18:31–34 (see also Mark 10:32–34). Summarize what Jesus said to the disciples:

READ JOHN 1:9–11 IN THE MARGIN.

I love how John described the rejection of Jesus. You can almost hear John's exasperation.

Later in his gospel, John told us, "Though he had done so many signs before them, they still did not believe in him, so that the word spoken by the prophet Isaiah might be fulfilled: 'Lord, who has believed what he heard from us, and to whom has the arm of the Lord been revealed?'" (John 12:37–38).

Jesus is a great example that you can't judge a book by its cover! He was not what the Jews were expecting. Remember the very first passage we studied: "In that day the branch of the Lord shall be beautiful and glorious, and the fruit of the land shall be the pride and honor of the survivors of Israel" (Isa. 4:2). The Jewish people were waiting for something beautiful and glorious to save their nation.

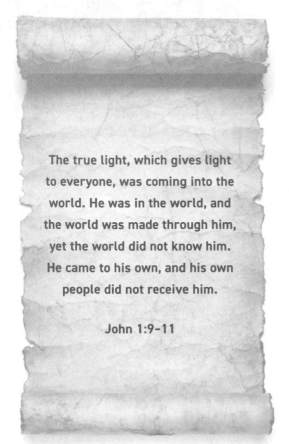

The true light, which gives light to everyone, was coming into the world. He was in the world, and the world was made through him, yet the world did not know him. He came to his own, and his own people did not receive him.

John 1:9-11

The nation of Israel was expecting world domination. Remember Isaiah 9:6–7 said the government shall be upon His shoulder and the increase of His government and of peace would have no end—from this time to forevermore.

Yet, when Jesus was born, He appeared to be a typical baby boy. Even though paintings might show a halo around His head or a light reflecting off His face, there was nothing special about the appearance of Jesus. In fact, after being told that the One the prophets spoke of (see they were expecting Him!), one of the apostles asked, "Can anything good come out of Nazareth?" Can you hear the scorn in this question? Read the scene in John 1:43–46.

Nathanael didn't believe this man was *the* One when he saw Jesus . . . until there was more proof when Jesus told Nathanael what he was doing when his brother found him sitting under the fig tree. See John 10:47–51.

I'd love for you to notice a pattern taking place through this study: Jesus did not hide who He was. Jesus told the Jewish people often and in many different ways that He was the Messiah. They just couldn't hear Him because they saw His human hands and feet, His ordinary clothing, and His worn sandals. I also suspect they felt threatened by His purity and power.

Is there someone in your life who immediately makes you defensive? Why do you think you respond to this person by getting your hackles up? Write about this relationship:

Perhaps this person is shedding a light of truth you don't want to acknowledge. Or perhaps this person makes you remember a past shame you aren't letting the blood of Christ wash away.

How could you try to react differently around this person?

Let's flip this around. Is there someone in your life who immediately gets defensive when *you're* around?

Is there someone who attacks you or always tries to drag you down, pointing out your faults?

Write about this relationship:

Perhaps this person is intimidated or uncomfortable around your "light." Or perhaps this person is holding on to shame that involves you somehow. How could you show forgiveness or more grace to this person?

Read John 10:22–39 and summarize the scene here:

Jesus was rejected precisely *because* there was nothing special about Him. He was just a man to the Jewish people. An ordinary Jewish man who claimed to be the Son of God.

WHAT'S THE POINT?

I think the point is to take a look at our own reactions to Jesus. For most of my life, I had the wrong impression of Jesus. It wasn't the same type of wrong impression as the Jews held, but it was a wrong impression nonetheless. When I was very young, I had a view of Jesus as someone who held up a rule book and made a record of every violation I made every single day. As I grew, I began to question whether Jesus was really God. In fact, I remember saying to a pastor that I thought Jesus walked the planet and was probably a good human being and a charismatic speaker, but likely nothing more.

Jesus didn't fit my picture of God, so I rejected Him too. The picture I had of God was one of power, but not one of love and grace. When I bothered to think about God at all, I couldn't make sense of a God who was a loving Creator who would "doom" millions of His creation to hell . . . forever. Didn't make sense. So, I decided not to try.

Take some time and reflect on the reactions you recall initially having about God and Jesus. What were those ideas?

Have those ideas changed? How so? What happened to shift those expectations?

HOW DO WE USE IT?

I tend to get defensive when something doesn't make sense to me. I also can easily get defensive when someone tells me I'm wrong or off base. Anyone else? A defensive posture creeps up in my heart when I see hypocrisy in people. If we think about it, there are a lot of things that can go wrong when we're trying to explain Jesus to others! Most of the time, they already have a picture of Jesus or God in their mind—and they won't accept that their picture isn't valid or correct.

How do we convince or challenge others to shed their preconceived notions of Jesus? Of God?

One way that I think is powerful to change someone's mindset is showing them how we used to view God and Jesus. People need to hear why we changed our minds. Please don't stop talking until you've described how much better your life is now!

You won't be ready to do this unless you've prepared. So, end today by writing how your life is different, so much better, with a correct view of Jesus and God:

Substitute and Silent Servant

ISAIAH 53:4–9

We've come to the place in our study where Jesus steps in front of us and takes our punishment. Remember, it's not a pardon. Someone died in our place. This is it. In Isaiah 53:4–9, we see the substitutionary atonement for our sins. One commentator said it this way: "Here is proclaimed to the whole world for all time the way by which a holy God can justify rebellious sinners and still be just."[5]

MARK UP ISAIAH 53:4–9 IN YOUR BIBLE. Once again, Jesus Himself declared this passage of Isaiah fulfilled through Him. Read Luke 22:37 in the margin.

Two other New Testament passages declare this passage of Scripture fulfilled through Jesus. Read about Jesus healing Peter's mother-in-law in Matthew 8:14–17 and read how Philip tied this

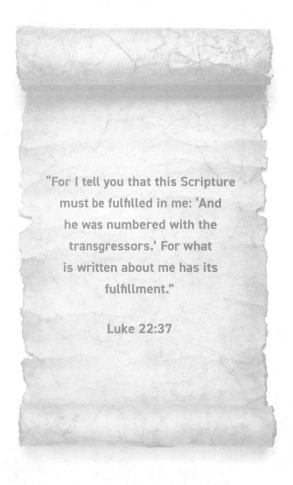

"For I tell you that this Scripture must be fulfilled in me: 'And he was numbered with the transgressors.' For what is written about me has its fulfillment."

Luke 22:37

passage of Isaiah to Jesus when explaining Christ to the Ethiopian eunuch in Acts 8:29–35.

I think Peter did an excellent job of tying Isaiah's words about Jesus being "pierced for our transgressions" and "crushed for our iniquities" so that "upon him was the chastisement that brought us peace, and with his wounds we are healed" (Isa. 53:5).

Read 1 Peter 2:21–25 and write the words that strike your heart the most:

Both 1 Corinthians 15:3–5 and Hebrews 9:24–28 also explain why and how Jesus died for our sins, in fulfillment of Isaiah 53:4–9.

Before God rescued the Jews from slavery in Egypt, a lamb was slain for each Jewish family. Its blood was marked on the family's door as the sign for the angel of death to pass over that household: hence the Passover. The slaying of an innocent as the substitute lifeblood for a person's sins was at the heart of the Jewish faith. The Jews would have understood completely the concept of substitutionary atonement for the forgiveness of sins. They had been doing it with animal sacrifices for centuries before Jesus was born.

Yet, they didn't see it in Jesus. They didn't hear it when He told them. They didn't believe it when the miracles happened every time Jesus showed up. When sickness, blindness, and even death were overcome by Jesus, they still didn't see it.

Do you? Do you get it? Can you write why or why not?

Please don't mistake the silence of Jesus to be weakness. Read Matthew 27:11–14 and write how Jesus responded to the "chief priests and elders":

"He gave _____ _____" (v. 12). (See also Matt. 26:62–63; Mark 14:55–62; 15:1–5; Luke 23:6–9; and John 19:6–11).

I would encourage you to read the whole account of the arrest and trial of Jesus in John 18 and 19. Jesus was resolute, determined, and willing to go to the cross. He was no victim of circumstances or evil people.

Jesus was fulfilling the Scriptures when He stood silent during His trial. I can't help wondering if He was thinking that His silence might trigger some Jewish leaders to remember the words of Isaiah as He stood before them. Perhaps even then the Holy Spirit was nudging people toward understanding what Jesus was doing.

Our God is a purposeful God. He doesn't waste any pain. Jesus taking these false accusations and ridicule in silence had a purpose. I can almost feel Jesus willing them to realize and submit to Him as their Messiah as I read the gospel of John.

One final note that Dr. Warren Wiersbe brought to my attention:

> The burial of Jesus Christ is as much a part of the gospel as is His death (1 Cor. 15:1–5), for the burial is proof that He actually died. The Roman authorities would not have released the body to Joseph and Nicodemus if the victim had not been dead (John 19:38–42; Mark 15:42–47).[6]

Isaiah told us the details of the arrest, trial, crucifixion, and death, all the way to the place of His burial in a rich man's tomb. Read Matthew 27:57–60 in the margin on the next page and circle "a rich man" and underline "laid it in his own new tomb."

If you didn't believe Isaiah 53 was about Jesus before, do you believe it now? Journal your confidence or doubts here:

> When it was evening, there came *a rich man* from Arimathea, named Joseph, who also was a disciple of Jesus. He went to Pilate and asked for *the body of Jesus.* Then Pilate ordered it to be given to him. And Joseph took the body and wrapped it in a clean linen shroud *and laid it in his own new tomb*, which he had cut in the rock. And he rolled a great stone to the entrance of the tomb and went away.
>
> Matthew 27:57–60

WHAT'S THE POINT?

In one verse we see it spelled out four different ways: Jesus was *pierced* for *our* transgressions, He was *crushed* for *our* iniquities, upon Him was the *chastisement* that brought *us* peace, and with His *wounds we* are healed (Isa. 53:5).

Do you hear that, sweet sister? We are healed. *You* are *healed* through the death of Jesus.

Write "I am healed" below:

In case you're feeling a bit unworthy of Jesus taking on all your sins, remember this: **All** of us, like sheep, have gone astray; we have turned—*every single one*—to her own way; and God has laid on Jesus the iniquity of us **all** (see Isa. 53:6).

None of us are worthy. Only the Lamb is worthy. *All* of us, every one of us, have gone her own way and away from God. But Jesus has taken every step away and turned it back around to God.

HOW DO WE USE IT?

Read Matthew 9:35–38 and describe the actions of Jesus:

> And Jesus went throughout all the cities and villages, teaching
> in their synagogues and proclaiming the gospel of the kingdom
> and healing every disease and every affliction. When he saw the
> crowds, he had compassion for them, because they were harassed
> and helpless, like sheep without a shepherd. Then he said to
> his disciples, "The harvest is plentiful, but the laborers are few;
> therefore pray earnestly to the Lord of the harvest to send out
> laborers into his harvest."

Write what Jesus said to His disciples:

"The harvest is _____, but the _____ ____ ____; therefore, _____ earnestly to the _____ of the harvest to _____ ____ _____ into ____ harvest."

We should go out into our communities and our cities and bring the good news of Jesus. We should try to help the physical needs of people who are hurting. We should have more compassion for others. We should never forget that we *all* have strayed and sinned before God.

And if our labor is difficult and we suffer in this life or struggle in our service to the Lord, shouldn't we try to be like Jesus—willing to do the will of the Father, no matter what?

Saving Servant

ISAIAH 53:10–12

F. B. Meyer, writer, pastor, and evangelist, said, "There is only one brow upon which this crown of thorns will fit. It is Jesus of Nazareth, who suffered innocently, died vicariously, was raised gloriously, and will return triumphantly, just as Isaiah foretold."[7]

I pray you are not losing your awe and wonder at these ancient words! The last section is the heart of the gospel in the Old Testament and so beautifully demonstrates the heart of our glorious God. Be amazed, sweet friend, be amazed as you study today.

MARK UP ISAIAH 53:10–12 IN YOUR BIBLE. Yesterday, we already studied how Jesus told us that He would be numbered with our transgressions so that Scripture would be fulfilled in Him. Isaiah 53 ends with an explanation of the cross from God's point of view.[8]

Have you ever considered the cross from God the Father's point of view? Take a few minutes and write about that here:

Some translations say God was "pleased" to crush Jesus with the weight of our sins, but the Hebrew word used can also mean "willed" or "purposed," and the grammatical structure of the sentence points more toward purposeful than pleased.[9] The death of Jesus, bearing the weight of our sin, certainly was purposeful.

Read John 10:9–18 and summarize how Jesus explains His mission and how He accepted the assignment from God the Father:

Jesus did not leave His glory behind to die on that cross for no purpose. The purpose was you!

He had you in mind on His way to the cross. How do I know that? Jesus told you Himself when He prayed for you just moments before His arrest. I can hear the plea in Jesus' voice as He asks the Father to take care of you:

> "*I do not ask for these only, but also for those who will believe in me through their word*, that they may all be one, just as you, Father, are in me, and I in you, that they also may be in us, so that the world may believe that you have sent me. The glory that you have given me I have given to them, that they may be one even as we are one, I in them and you in me, that they may become perfectly one, so that the world may know that you sent me and loved them even as you loved me. Father, I desire that they also, whom you have given me, may be with me where I am, to see my glory that you have given me because you loved me before the foundation of the world." (John 17:20–24)

The five verses are about you because you believed in Jesus (although indirectly) because of the ministry of the apostles. Read the passage above again if you need to. Hear all that Jesus asked the Father for you: may all be one, glory, become perfectly one, be with Jesus in heaven ("where I am").

God was purposeful in sending Jesus to take your sins so that the Holy One of Israel could be reconciled with you, in relationship with you. You are *that* important to Him! He would suffer, even to death under the weight of *all* your sins, because He loves you (remember Isa. 53:10!).

Do you feel *that* important to God? Why or why not?

Whether you feel it or not, it's the hard truth. God loves you enough to have His own Son die for you. It's hard to picture someone else dying for you. We can't wrap our minds around it, so we must use our hearts and souls. Our hearts and souls long for a love so pure and complete, love that would unflinchingly endure anything and everything to spare us, to keep our relationship. We long for it because it's *real*. Such love exists. In. God. Alone.

Only God. Only Jesus. Love complete.

Don't worry. Our amazing God will not leave His Son, Jesus, crushed on the cross! Jesus will prosper and His days will be prolonged because of the resurrection. When Jesus rose from the dead, He fulfilled the prophecy of Isaiah 53:10–12. Jesus continues to "prolong His days" (v. 10) as He lives forever at the right hand of God, interceding on your behalf.

How would you ask Jesus to intercede for you right now? If you are important enough to die for, believe that He longs to hear your struggles and desires to help you with your difficulties. Write them here and expect that He'll remain working for you:

WHAT'S THE POINT?

"It is finished!" (John 19:30).

The point of the final verses in Isaiah 53 is the ending to the story of all human-kind. The point of verses 10–12 is to tell us the end of the story. God would save us from the enemy, from sin, once and for all. When this work is finished, as Jesus cried out from the cross, Jesus would rise from the dead in victory, and take His rightful place on the throne next to His Father. Jesus will remain there, interceding for us, until it is time for His return.

These final verses also answer the "why" questions.

Why did Jesus have to die on the cross? To bear our sins and be our substitute. A holy and just God could not simply pardon sin. The penalty had to be paid (life-blood will be required: Gen. 9:5).

Why will Jesus look and be satisfied after the "anguish of his soul"? Because those who have knowledge of Him will be made righteous before God, and many will be saved.

Why would God allow His one and only Son to suffer such agony? Because Jesus was willing to be the perfect sacrifice/substitute so that many of their children (that's us!) could be returned to God, and out of the grips of the enemy.

HOW DO WE USE IT?

First we ask this great question: "Am I satisfied with that which the Lord Jesus did for me upon the cross?"[10]

After studying all that Jesus endured—tortured nearly to death, then a horrible death on the cross—knowing He was the Son of God, knowing He had every right to sit on the throne in heaven, how can we *not* be satisfied with what He did for us?

Do you feel that you are completely forgiven, totally washed clean of all your sins for all time? Before you answer, consider that almighty God, the Ancient of Days, saw Jesus on that cross and was satisfied that your punishment was fulfilled.

What holds you back from living in an attitude before God that you have been completely forgiven?

The next time you begin to tear yourself down, doubt your worth, question your fate for eternity, please, I beg you, consider the cross. Reread Isaiah 53. Remind yourself what Jesus took from you. And friend, He's never given it back. And He never will.

Write the three most common ways you tend to doubt yourself, question your worth, or feel unsure of your salvation:

We stand forgiven. It is finished. We *will* see Jesus in the glorious eternity God has planned for us (we're studying that next!).

Second, fully comprehending our abundant blessings through Jesus, we strive to live a Christlike life, a Jesus-first life, a humble-servant life:

> Do nothing from selfish ambition or conceit, but in humility count others more significant than yourselves. Let each of you look not only to his own interests, but also to the interests of others. (Phil. 2:3–4)

How could you honor the work and suffering of Jesus by humbly serving others? See if you can list a few you are doing already, but then add one or two more areas where you could consider others more significant than yourself:

As we close this most specific prophecy regarding Jesus in the book of Isaiah, take a moment to reflect on the fact that this single chapter is enough evidence to declare that the Bible is true and powerful.

Write your thoughts about the truth of the Bible here:

Review, Reflect, and Pray

Go back through the lessons and highlight the prophecies that had the most impact on you this week. Write the "address" of those prophecies here ("address" example: Isaiah 26:3):

Go back through the lessons and put a big question mark in the margin beside anything that you still have questions or doubts about, or where you want to learn more.

Write a prayer of thanks, make a request for humility, and petition our Intercessor for help:

Week Five:
The Savior's Sacrifice

GROUP DISCUSSION OR REFLECTION QUESTIONS

1. Reflect on these ten prophecies from Isaiah 53 as set forth in *The Moody Bible Commentary.*[11] Discuss what you learned or what impacted you about each one:

   Jesus suffered an appalling, disfiguring death (52:14).

   Jesus' blood sprinkled nations and brought kings to submission (52:15).

   Jesus was rejected by Israel for being too plain (53:1–3).

   Jesus' suffering was considered to be punishment for His sin by Israel (53:4–6).

   Jesus suffered and died without resistance, accepting God's will to provide atonement for Israel and the world (53:7–8).

   Jesus was buried in a rich man's tomb (53:9).

   Jesus was resurrected from the dead (53:10–11).

   Jesus was given innumerable followers (spiritual followers) (53:10).

   Jesus is satisfied today with the forgiveness His death provided (53:11).

   Jesus has been rewarded by God the Father as the victor over sin (53:12).

2. How does the horrific nature of the death of Jesus make you feel?

3. How do you react to Jesus' dying without resistance and without defending Himself?

4. Where is Jesus now? What is His position? What is He doing?

5. Thinking about the difficult life and death of Jesus, how can He understand and intercede for the difficult circumstances in your life?

6. How can we honor the sacrifice of Jesus in our lives today?

THE SAVIOR'S EVERLASTING PEACE

This final week will wrap up the messianic prophecies about the first coming of Christ, and look forward to some prophecies about our Messiah's second coming. We will study Isaiah 55 and how the Word of God is purposeful, personal, and powerful. We'll study Isaiah 61 and the triumphant declaration of Jesus that Isaiah's prophecy was fulfilled through Him. Finally, we'll take a glimpse at the future promises of a glorious eternal life.

Without Cost

ISAIAH 55

Isaiah 55 was another pivotal chapter in my faith journey. This critical turning point had to do with whether the Bible was the inspired Word of God or just a collection of writings by some ancient men. Growing up, the Bible was not something my family read outside of the printed passages in a booklet at church on Sunday mornings. My whole life, I struggled to understand why the Bible was so important. I even recall telling someone that old, white guys wrote it thousands of years ago, with their own opinions and biases, and thus, it could not be the "Word of God." That person asked me whether I thought a mere man could write something different than what God wanted him to write. Without hesitation, I replied, "Of course! That's why it's called free will." Duh. It's just a book. I rejected it outright as ancient and inapplicable.

After Austin died and I received my very first Bible, I began attending a church where everyone brought their own Bibles. We stood when we read from it, and it was considered the unerring Word of God, God-breathed, and the ultimate authority in our lives. Needless to say, I was a bit skeptical. To be honest, I was also a bit intimidated. I didn't know much about this Bible stuff.

As the pastor visited our house to minister to us in those early days after we lost our son, I recall every detail of one particular conversation. Pastor Steve boldly announced in my kitchen that the Holy Spirit was a gift to every believer and that the Holy Spirit is how the Bible came alive, how a person without the Holy Spirit likely wouldn't get much out of the Bible. I was listening. He said the Holy Spirit helps believers understand the Word of God.

He said it so matter-of-factly that it almost sounded like a "double-dog-dare-you" to me! Or like that old commercial "just try it, you'll like it!" I couldn't resist this challenge. I began to read my Bible with a skeptical, "I'll have to see it before I believe it" kind of attitude. I was told to begin my Bible reading in the gospel of John, and so that's what I did.

And then it happened.

It happened to me.

The Holy Spirit brought revelation to my heart and my mind. The Word of God became alive and powerful in my hands through the work of the Holy Spirit. I couldn't believe it. I kept it quiet for a while. For months I pored over the sacred Scriptures, alternating between awe and sorrow, desperation and peace. I couldn't believe everything was right there in black and white. It had been there my whole life. Power. Peace. Answers. GOD. Showing His mighty face and heart to a mere human. To me.

The Bible became my lifeline, my peace, my comfort. When later I felt God calling me to be a Bible teacher, I spent a lot of time asking Him how was I going to teach other women *how* this Bible thing worked. I wondered, "How am I going to share what happens to me when I read my Bible without sounding crazy?"

I happened to be studying the book of Isaiah at that time. I'll never forget it. It's another scene I can still see perfectly in my mind: it was a very tough grieving week for my son, and I sought solitude and silence and privacy to weep the gut-deep sobs of a shattered mom. I went out to the hiking trails near our Arizona home. I walked for a while. Cried through most of it. Finally dug my Bible out of my car and found a picnic table. Even in the midst of my deep sorrow, I felt God pressing on my heart to be a Bible teacher and help women understand its power.

"How?!" I said it out loud, a frustrated, tired, and sad voice, lashing out in my anguish. "People will think I'm crazy, that I've lost my mind in my grief."

"Maybe you're crazy and this doesn't happen to every Christian," said a voice inside my mind. "Maybe I am," I agreed. Then I opened my Bible, with my bookmark at Isaiah 55, and I began to read.

Isaiah 55 opens very swiftly with words of Jesus and the free gift of salvation. Again, I wondered why I went my whole life thinking I had to work so hard to get to heaven. Chapter 55 then shifts to the verses I'd already heard from other believers quite often in my early Christian walk: "My ways are not your ways, my thoughts are higher than your thoughts." People actually say these words to the grieving mother quite often.

I rolled my angry eyes at those words—*whatever*! I skimmed over them with some annoyance. It doesn't really help my grief to know that God understands or knows why I have to go through the rest of my life without my son.

But then God did a thing. I could feel the air still around me, even though I was outside, as I read the next lines. The Holy Spirit washed over me in such a revelation that I wept, right there at that picnic table, for several long minutes. No longer in grief, but rather completely overwhelmed by a God who would take a moment to lift His daughter's chin to look into His mighty face and hear the answer to what she was seeking.

I'm going to leave a placeholder here and let you study Isaiah 55 for yourself. Ask your own questions, ponder the ancient words, seek the Holy Spirit, and enjoy your own answers today. Don't worry. I'll finish the story when you're finished.

Mark up Isaiah 55 in your Bible. How was God's Word described in Isaiah 55? Write what you discovered:

Now that you've had time to do your own searching with the Lord, I'll share what God revealed to me that day. I was searching for a way to explain to others *how* the Bible was so powerful. The Lord showed me that the Bible is purposeful, personal, and powerful.

Purposeful: Scripture is purposeful because it was provided for a purpose (like the rain or the snow, to water the earth), it was given to us for instruction, guidance, comfort, and so on—for a purpose—and it works because it was sent for these specific purposes. The Bible has a job to do and it will do it (it will not return empty).

Personal: The Scriptures are personal; giving each believer what she needs, when she needs it (seed to the sower, bread to the eater). How these verses struck me that day likely didn't strike you the same way. In fact, these same verses struck me differently a couple years later (they were pointing to Jesus, which is what *I* needed at *that* time).

Powerful: The Word of God has the power to bring good change (it will succeed in the purpose for which God sent it), the power to bring joy and peace, and the power to bring blessings (go out in joy, led forth in peace; mountains sing, trees clap; good crops instead of thorns). The Word of God will stand forever (an everlasting sign that will not be cut off). "Heaven and earth will pass away, but my words will not pass away," said Jesus in Matthew 24:35.

The Word of God is truly living and working in our lives. I can't explain the supernatural power of it, but I can testify to its powerful work in my life. Can you?

Write about your experiences with the power of Scripture here:

WHAT'S THE POINT?

Three things are key in this passage. First, salvation is the work of God, offered freely to those who turn to Him. Read John 5:24 in the margin, and circle "hears" and "believes" and underline "eternal life." Jesus said,

Have you accepted this free gift? If yes, can you write about the day you turned to Jesus for salvation? If not yet, can you write what's holding you back?

"Truly, truly, I say to you, whoever hears my word and believes him who sent me has eternal life. He does not come into judgment, but has passed from death to life."

John 5:24

Second, the Davidic covenant was fulfilled by Jesus Christ, a descendant of David (see Matthew 1 for the genealogy of Jesus), who will forever be on the throne.

Do you have any doubts that Jesus fulfilled God's promise to David that his descendant would sit on the throne forever? Write why or why not:

Third, one scholar put it this way: "God sends forth his word by the power of the Holy Spirit. It makes a circular trip like the cycle of precipitation: 'For from him and through him and [back] to him are all things' (Rom 11:36)."[1]

HOW DO WE USE IT?

First, we realize that we're starving without Jesus and turn to Him. Second, we acknowledge that Jesus is the promised Messiah and our Lord and Savior. Third, we treat the Word of God like the nourishment it is meant to give us: like rain and snow to the earth, we *need* the Word of God to survive. We need to be using the Word of God to nourish our souls, allowing it to do the work God sent it to do in our hearts.

How much are you allowing the Word of God to change you?

When was the last time the Word of God provoked a change in your attitude, your behavior, or your life in some way? Write about it:

Sweet friend, I pray that we never stop allowing the Word of God to change us!

Because Jesus Said So

ISAIAH 61

Today, we'll cover the triumphant moment when Jesus announced that Isaiah 61, verse 1 and part of verse 2, had been fulfilled by Him that very day. It was a "drop the mic" kind of moment!

We will study our final messianic prophecy together in the first verses of Isaiah 61, but then we'll continue on with Isaiah 61 because the remaining verses are also prophecy. The remaining verses relate to the second coming of Jesus. Now don't panic! End times prophecies are not any different than the messianic prophecies we've been studying. These prophecies just haven't been fulfilled *yet*.

That being said, let's start with Jesus' triumphant moment.

MARK UP ISAIAH 61:1–2 IN YOUR BIBLE. Next, read Luke 4:16–21 and try to picture the scene at the synagogue that day. Use the vision of your own church if you can't picture a Jewish synagogue. Picture at least one hundred (likely more) men gathered, sitting silently to listen to one man standing among them. Try to take in the words Jesus spoke in that powerful moment.

Since we're looking for *Jesus* in the ancient words of Isaiah, you might have missed the reference to the Holy Trinity in verse 1. I know that I missed it until several commentaries pointed it out. Read verse 1 again and see if you can figure out how this verse involves all three members of the Trinity.

Isaiah 61 opens with "the Spirit of the Lord GOD is upon me, because the LORD has anointed me. . . ." The Spirit is the Holy Spirit. The Lord GOD is the Father, and the person speaking is the Servant, Jesus. The Hebrew word for Messiah is the same word used for "anointed" in verse 1. Anointed means that a person was chosen and appointed for a special purpose.[2]

How would you feel about someone standing up in your church, holding a writing that was centuries old, and declaring the writing was about *her*, that *she* was the person who would do the great things written more than six hundred years ago? Skeptical? Are you thinking, "Poor thing, she's lost her mind"? I bet you wouldn't naturally think, "Well, there you are! We've been watching and waiting for you!"

It seems natural for the Jewish people to scorn Jesus after He declared Isaiah 61:1 and part of verse 2 was fulfilled that very day, right in their midst, by Him.

Do you think you would have responded differently? Why or why not?

Please notice that Jesus did not announce the end of the Jewish faith. Jesus announced their future and the next step in Israel's journey with God.[3] I recall a message I heard several years ago that warned Christians against thinking poorly of Israel and Judaism. The pastor reminded us that the Jewish people are God's chosen people, our ancestry, part of our family as children of God.

The Jewish people are part of *our* story as Christ followers. God has great plans for the Jewish people. Hence, why I want you to read *the rest* of Isaiah 61 in a few minutes. Many of the Jewish people will ultimately turn to Jesus Christ as the Messiah. The nation of Israel will be restored to the glory God intended for it. Yes, we'll be a part of that.

As part of the story, we Christians need to be praying for the Jewish people and praying for the nation of Israel. I am praying for hearts to be softened and minds to be opened to the Scriptures and Jesus' fulfillment of those prophecies.

Have you ever prayed for the nation of Israel or the Jewish people? Write about it here:

WHAT'S THE POINT?

If we read carefully, we'll notice that Jesus was *not* told what passage to read out of the Isaiah scroll. Luke 4 tells us that Jesus stood up to read (as traditionally someone would do) and the scroll of Isaiah was handed to Him. Next, "He unrolled the scroll *and found the place* where it was written" (v. 17) and began reading out loud. Jesus chose these two verses specifically to announce who He was and state that He would fulfill His mission: to bring good news to the poor, to bind up the brokenhearted, to proclaim liberty to the captives, and to open the prison of those who are bound (see Isa. 61:1).

He read one more line ("to proclaim the year of the Lord's favor") and then said the passage had been fulfilled in their hearing on that very day. Boom! Mic drop (or hand the scroll back to the attendant). Sit down. Jesus waited until *all* eyes were on Him before He made His big announcement.

Interestingly, the first reaction is positive. The very next verse in Luke says: "And all spoke well of him and marveled at the gracious words that were coming from his mouth" (v. 22). In Matthew's gospel we're told the same: Jesus' fame spread throughout the land.

> And [Jesus] went throughout all Galilee, teaching in their
> synagogues and proclaiming the gospel of the kingdom and healing
> every disease and every affliction among the people. So his fame
> spread throughout all Syria, and they brought him all the sick,
> those afflicted with various diseases and pains, those oppressed by
> demons, those having seizures, and paralytics, and he healed them.
> (Matt. 4:23–24)

It wasn't until later, when the Jewish leaders grasped the power and popularity of Jesus, that they became jealous and scared of losing their status and power.

Have you ever initially liked someone, but became jealous of her later? Maybe it's difficult to admit, but it's worth asking yourself the question. If you can say yes to this question (as I can), write a prayer of repentance for yourself and a prayer of intercession for the Jewish people:

We must also note that Jesus stopped mid-verse: to proclaim the year of the Lord's favor. Jesus stopped reading halfway through verse 2! The second half of verse 2 says, "And the day of vengeance of our God; to comfort all who mourn" (Isa. 61:2).

Why do you think Jesus stopped at that point?

One commentary states, "That Jesus stopped reading after the words 'favorable year' and did not go on to read 'day of vengeance' indicates a clear distinction between His first and second comings."[4]

I think this conclusion is probably accurate, but I also think that Jesus was a master teacher. He knew His audience. The men sitting in the synagogue that day likely could finish verse 2 for themselves. Jesus purposefully left a cliffhanger for His audience to grasp onto and form their own conclusions. When teaching, it is said that self-discovery is the highest form of learning. I think Jesus stopped at this point both to emphasize that only part of Isaiah 61 was being fulfilled at that time *and* to allow the audience to think for themselves, to study the Scriptures for themselves, and to take the actions and words of Jesus in light of Isaiah 61 and realize—of their own minds and hearts—that Jesus was the Messiah and that the day of vengeance was coming.

Once they put two and two together, the remaining verses of Isaiah 61 would tumble quickly into place, the double blessing that the Lord will bestow on His beloved Israel once she turned to Jesus. One day, Israel will be restored to the glorious plans God had for His people.

Ponder what a glorious day that will be as you mark up Isaiah 61:3–11 in your Bible. What part of the glorious restoration gives you the most hope, peace, or comfort?

HOW DO WE USE IT?

Isaiah 61 and Luke 4 can become a bedrock, a solid foundation, for our belief in prophecy and in the absolute truth of the Bible as God's Word. Only God could have made all these predictions *more than half a millennium* before they took place! Only the Anointed One, the Messiah, could have stood in that synagogue and declared that Isaiah's prophecies were fulfilled by Him.

If you believe in Jesus as your Savior and Lord, then His own declaration should be enough to remove any doubt that the book of Isaiah predicted Jesus long before His arrival on earth.

We use Isaiah 61 and Luke 4 to stand resolute upon the Scriptures. Declaring the Bible as truth and authority for our lives is becoming increasingly difficult in our culture. Nevertheless, we boldly declare our faith in Jesus. We stay steadfast, clinging to the Bible as the authority from God Himself. We study, pray, and talk about the Bible. We stand together as women who hold up the Bible as a lens to our lives.

How could you *use* the Bible more in your life? I'm not talking about making more time to read it or study the Word. I'm talking about finding practical applications in your daily life, in your family, in your home, in your community.

Give yourself a few minutes to brainstorm, meaning there are no bad or incorrect ideas and you should write anything that pops into your mind:

Now, a more difficult question: If you believe, without a doubt, that the Bible is the Word of God, then how is it *changing* you? How *could* it change you? Same instructions: give yourself a few minutes to brainstorm, meaning there are no bad ideas and you should write anything that pops into your mind:

No More Tears

ISAIAH 65:17–25; REVELATION 21:1–6

Now that we've spent six weeks together looking backward at ancient prophecy and the life of Jesus, let's close our time together by looking *forward*.

Something we didn't note yesterday is this: Jesus brought the "year" of the Lord—a long time of grace and second chances. Please notice that God only gave Himself a "day" for "vengeance" (Isa. 61:2). Isn't that just like the God we've come to know through the ancient prophecies of Isaiah? He is mighty to save. He is patient and compassionate.

But that isn't all. He is just and pure and holy and righteous. And He keeps His word. If He says it, He's going to do it. The consequences spoken by the Lord in Isaiah also *will* come to pass. Don't skip over them because they sound unpleasant. Don't skim the harsh language. Try to picture the destruction. We must be stirred to action. We must do our part to reduce the number of people who will face these dire consequences. We must heed *both* parts of Isaiah, the glorious restoration of Jerusalem and our eternal lives, and the eternal hell others will face if they reject the Son.

But that is not how we are going to finish this study! We are going to study passages that help this grieving mama grasp onto joy and peace each day: this earth, this life, will not last forever. There will be an end to my pain and to yours. There will be a new heaven and a new earth—where there will be no more sorrow, no more pain. No. More. Tears.

MARK UP ISAIAH 65:17–25 IN YOUR BIBLE. Next, turn to Revelation 21:1–6 and mark up the vision given to the apostle John (the disciple whom Jesus loved).

There will no longer be any sea. That makes me a bit sad because I love the ocean, but a world where mankind can once again dwell with God and "God Himself will be among them" (Rev. 21:3 NASB), is a much better place!

Verse 4 is well-known and often quoted, but please don't let its familiarity take away from the promises. I'm going to put the promises God has spoken to us in verse 4 below.

I'd like you to journal under each one what the fulfillment of each promise would look and feel like for you personally:

God Himself will wipe away *every* tear from [your] eyes:

there will no longer be any death:

there will no longer be any mourning:

there will no longer be any crying:

there will no longer be any pain:

the former things [your old life] have passed away:

Let's go ahead and add the next promise in verse 5:

Behold, [God] is making *all* things new:

Sister in Christ, please dwell here a bit and get this settled in your heart and your mind: these promises *will* come true. The Bible is not a fairy tale, or just a nice story. It's truth. It's God's Word. It is God-breathed. Everything you wrote above *will* come true. Someday. Someday we will experience the new heaven and the new earth.

Next, God tells John to write all this down! He said to John, "Write, for these words are faithful and true" (Rev. 21:5 NASB). And just to make sure we cannot misunderstand who He is or what His mission was about, next Jesus said: "It is done. I am the Alpha and the Omega, the beginning and the end. I will give water to the one who thirsts from the spring of the water of life, without cost" (Rev. 21:6 NASB).

Jesus has done it. It is finished (John 19:30). Jesus was there in the beginning and He will be there when this world comes to an end. But while we're waiting, He will give eternal life without cost. We can't earn it. We can't take it. We can't create it. The Giver of Life *will* give it to the one who thirsts for it, who receives it, who drinks it. Jesus. Believe in Him, enjoy eternal life in God's glory—without cost. So simple, yet so true.

By now, near the end of this study, I hope you are comfortable declaring that God speaks to us through the Bible. Jesus said so. The words in the book say so. Now, will you say so?

Write why you feel confident or why you're still hesitating (which is okay!):

If you are still hesitant or have questions, please seek out a mentor. Your questions and doubts are legitimate. Someone who is further along on their journey with Jesus may be able to help you. Also, keep wrestling with those questions. God *wants* you to understand and believe Him, so keep asking questions. Don't forget to listen for His still, small voice inside your heart. Take time to sit quietly before Him. Find a solitary place so that you can allow the silence to minister to your heart and your mind.

WHAT'S THE POINT?

The times described in Isaiah and Revelation are coming. We must work hard so that we do not get carried away with the worries of this world and forget that another world *is* coming. We must not lose sight of our inheritance. Glory and eternal life are coming. As sure as we can be about the fulfilled prophecies about Jesus in the book of Isaiah, we can be sure that a new heaven and a new earth await. Heaven and peace are coming and we will take part in eternal glory.

We also can't be afraid of prophecy. We must read it and study it. The prophecies that have yet to be fulfilled should be ready in our minds so that we may be able to recognize that what is happening around us may be God's will and according to God's plan.

Have you studied end times prophecies before? What was your experience? Or is this topic all new to you?

Would you like to study more end times prophecies? If so, can you think of someone to invite to study with you? Also, I would recommend that you ask your pastor for reliable sources to study that come from solid, biblically based writers. The internet is not necessarily a reliable place to gather resources on this topic.

HOW DO WE USE IT?

We use the prophecies that are yet to be fulfilled as a beacon. A beacon of hope. A reminder to keep our minds on the end of the story. We turn to end times prophecies to return a sense of urgency to our weary hearts. We remind ourselves that the best is yet to come. We stir ourselves into action to share the gospel with others so that none will be lost and everyone can find peace and joy through Christ. Sharing the gospel doesn't have to be initiating a conversation with a stranger about Jesus or handing out a tract in a park. For me, sharing the gospel means being willing to mention God, my prayers, my study of the Bible, or my church with the people in my life and at work. It's not against the law. Many people are mistaken in thinking the law prohibits them from sharing their faith at work. What the law requires is separation of church and state (the government). If you work for a private, non-government entity, there are no restrictions whatsoever about sharing your faith. When a coworker mentioned a news story, I mentioned that I've been praying about something similar. It opened a discussion about praying. A few months later, she brought a student to my office who had mentioned prayer and needed help. Although I didn't reach the coworker at that time, she connected me to a student who was open to talking about Jesus. Sharing the gospel is most natural for me when I'm connecting with someone and I can find a way to blend in how God impacts and influences my life. In light of how difficult this world is becoming, I am finding it easier and easier to weave God and Jesus into my relationships and conversations. People are hurting, so people are seeking. Let them see Jesus through you and your life.

How are you currently using end times prophecies to encourage your heart?

What reminders could you create to keep a sense of urgency and compassion for the lost?

Jesus Is Coming

REVELATION 22

Today, we'll study the very last prophecy in the Bible, Revelation 22. The English Standard Version (ESV) of the Bible has "The River of Life" and "Jesus Is Coming" as the headings in Revelation 22. Isn't it fitting that we should end our study of prophecies relating to the Messiah with "Jesus Is Coming"?

MARK UP REVELATION 22 IN YOUR BIBLE. Go slowly. As we did with the promises in Revelation 21:4, journal your way through the promises in Revelation 22. As you mark up the verses, write what your life will look like and feel like when this vision comes to pass. I'll give you a few prompts, but feel free to add whatever else comes to mind:

When you see the throne of God and the Lamb with a river of the water of life flowing from it:

When there is a tree of life, bearing fruit and with leaves that will heal the nations:

When there will no longer be any curse (no more sin; think of the garden of Eden prior to the curse of sin):

When you will see God face to face and serve Him alone:

When there will no longer be any day or night or sun because God will be your light:

When you will reign with God forever and ever:

Once again, God takes a pause and tells John, "These words are faithful and true" (Rev. 22:6 NASB).

Verses 7 and 12 begin with the same phrase. Write it below:

Behold, __ ___ _____ _____.

Does it feel to you like Jesus is coming quickly? I most often feel like a kid on a really long car ride, asking every five minutes, "Are we there yet?" Yes, sometimes I whine to God. I'm so ready for Jesus to come back and fix this broken world. I'm so ready to see my Austin.

What about you? Are you ready for Jesus to come back quickly? Write your initial reaction (don't edit it for what you think you should say!):

Verses 13 and 17 mirror some of the verses you studied yesterday. Jesus is the Alpha and the Omega, the beginning and the end. He will give the water of life without cost.

Fill in verse 20 below:

[Jesus] who testifies to these things says, "____ __ ___ _____ _____."

Next, write the rest of verse 20 as your response:

_____. _____, _____ _____!

Do you know what "Amen" means? Amen means "let it be done."

How can these final prophecies about our Messiah minister to you during this temporary life?

Let's close our lessons with the blessing of the very last line in your Bible:

May the grace of the Lord Jesus be with all. Amen!

Review, Reflect, and Pray

Go back through the lessons and highlight the prophecies that had the most impact on you this week. Write the "address" of those prophecies here ("address" example: Isaiah 26:3):

Go back through the lessons and put a big question mark in the margin beside anything that you still have questions or doubts about, or where you want to learn more.

Write a prayer about the rest of your life on earth. Write a prayer of praise for your eternal life in heaven:

Week Six:
The Savior's Everlasting Peace

GROUP DISCUSSION OR REFLECTION QUESTIONS

1. Do you struggle to rest in the grace and peace of God? Why or why not?

2. How will you keep focused on our glorious future?

3. Why should end times prophecies spur us into action?

4. What are you looking forward to the most in our eternal glory?

5. Is Jesus' declaration about Isaiah's prophecy in chapter 61 enough to declare *all* of the prophecies in Isaiah to be legitimate predictions from God Himself? Why do you think so?

6. What are your hesitations, questions, or doubts about prophecy?

7. Do you know women you could trust to ask questions about the Bible? Who are they?

8. Do you know someone who needs to come to faith in Jesus? Make a commitment to pray and interact with them today.

CLOSING EXERCISE

Before you close this study, I'd love to have you spend just one more hour to bring these lessons and insights "home" in your heart where they can influence change in your life. Reviewing information studied is one of the best ways to keep the lessons in our brains.

Gather some index cards and a highlighter. Next, please spend some time flipping back through this book. Review the notes you made. Read what you wrote. Highlight the information that has made an impact on you. Write Scripture on those index cards. Consider making these notecards:

Mark one index card "JESUS FULFILLED IT!" and write at least one prophecy of Isaiah that Jesus fulfilled; pick the prophecy that had the biggest impact on you, one that made you go, "Wow, I didn't know that" or "That's so cool!"

Fill one index card with changes you'd like to make in the way you approach Bible study.

Fill another card with changes you'd like to make in certain behaviors or attitudes in your home or at work.

Mark one index card with CONSEQUENCES and list the name of at least one person you could interact with who doesn't know Jesus yet.

Finally, take one last card, write GLORY in capital letters at the top, and add a verse that gives you hope for our future eternal glory. Your GLORY card can be your encouragement when this world feels too dark, too hard, too long. On the other side of the card, write, "If God said it, He's going to do it!"

CLOSING COMMENTS

Friend, you did it! You climbed Mount Everest and lived to tell about it. I hope you learned something new and gained insights that will impact your life and the lives of those around you. I pray you will always feel that Bible study and seeking the Lord are worth the effort. Remember, He is worthy of the work!

My prayer for you is that you will take this study not only into your churches and circles of Christian friends, but into those circles where Jesus is not yet known and the Bible is not seen as the precious and powerful tool that it can be for believers. May the Lord bless you and keep you as you use your knowledge of the prophecies predicting Jesus to bring the good news to the poor, proclaim liberty to the captives, and free the prisoners of sin. In the powerful name of Jesus, the One and Only Son of God, the Messiah, I pray all these things. Amen!

Thank you for the privilege of going on this journey through the ancient Scriptures with you! I treasured every single moment.

God bless you and yours,

Kim

kim@kimaerickson.com

WITH GREAT GRATITUDE

Head bowed, knees bent, I come before the throne room of the Ancient of Days to declare my great gratitude in His never-ending mercy toward me. For His power to hold each and every life in His hands with tenderness and love. For His patient pursuit of this sinner who needed her Savior. For His willingness to share Himself with us through His Word. For giving us prophecy so that we could grow to know Him and trust Him. Thank You, Father!

To Jesus, the Messiah, the Christ, the Son of God, thank You for knowing what was going to happen to You—and doing it anyway—for us, for me. Thank You for Your resolved determination to fulfill everything the prophets spoke about You!

To the Holy Spirit, my Helper, my Comforter, my Counselor, who makes revelation through the Holy Scriptures possible. Thank You for teaching me everything I needed to write this study!

To my husband, Devin, who doesn't fully comprehend the depths of my great gratitude for the privilege of sharing my life with him as my best friend and partner. Thank you, Dev, for being you and for always making me laugh!

To my son, Ethan, who brings me such joy and happiness with the incredible young man he is becoming. I'm so proud of you, E. Thanks for cheering me on and trying to keep me calm!

To Judy Dunagan, my acquisition editor at Moody Publishers, for believing in this project that took me many years to put into print. Thank you for your vision and dedication to women's Bible studies. Your heart for the Lord always comes through first, but I am so thankful for your keen mind and depth of knowledge of the Scriptures. Thank you, Judy, for trusting me with the prophecies of Isaiah!

To Pam Pugh, my developmental editor who has the ability to take what is written and make it better, more impactful. Thank you for tackling this study and honing it into something women can use and, hopefully, enjoy!

To the Moody team, my great gratitude for every single person who worked (and will continue to work) on this project. May you be blessed and find great joy in your work!

To the scholars who went before me through the ancient scrolls of Isaiah, I am forever in your debt. I have great gratitude for your hard work and writings that shed light on the words of Isaiah. I would not have appreciated or fully understood the depths and beauty of the prophecies of Isaiah without your help. Thank you for your work!

NOTES

GETTING STARTED

1. John N. Oswalt, *Isaiah: The NIV Application Commentary* (Grand Rapids: Zondervan, 2003), 455.

2. Michael Rydelnik and James Spencer, "Isaiah," in *The Moody Bible Commentary*, ed. Michael Rydelnik and Michael Vanlaningham (Chicago: Moody Publishers, 2014), 1006.

3. Isaiah prophesied numerous events and outcomes in history that came true. Some came true near in time to when Isaiah spoke them, but some came true *hundreds* of years later. It's astonishing. Some of these are:

   - Israel was conquered by the Assyrian army, and later Judah was conquered by the Babylonians, and Jerusalem was burned (Isa. 7; 5:13; 6:11–13).

   - Within sixty-five years, Ephraim (another name for Israel) would be captured by the Assyrian army, but that army would be stopped short of destroying Jerusalem, and in fact, would suddenly return to its own country (7:1–7; also see 2 Kings 17–19).

   - Because Judah's king refused to heed Isaiah's warnings, Judah would be overtaken as well (8:1–8).

   - The Medes attacked the Babylonians via Cyrus the Great (13:17–20).

   - Within three years, Moab would be destroyed (16:14).

   - Egypt would fall captive to the Assyrians (20:1–4).

WEEK ONE: THE SAVIOR IS COMING

1. Edward E. Hindson, "Isaiah 11:1–16," *The Moody Handbook of Messianic Prophecy: Studies and Expositions of the Messiah in the Old Testament*, ed. Michael Rydelnik and Edwin Blum (Chicago: Moody Publishers, 2019), 855.

2. J. Randall Price, "Isaiah 4:2," *The Moody Handbook of Messianic Prophecy*, 803.

3. Ibid., 803–4.

4. Ibid., 806–7.

5. Gary V. Smith, *Isaiah 1–39*, vol. 15A, New American Commentary (Nashville: B&H, 2007), 155–56.

6. Price, "Isaiah 4:2," 813.

7. See also Andrew M. Davis, *Exalting Jesus in Isaiah* (Nashville: Holman Reference, 2017), 27–28; John N. Oswalt, "Isaiah 4:2–6," in *Isaiah: The NIV Application Commentary*; *The Moody Bible Commentary* ed. Michael Rydelnik and Michael Vanlaningham (Chicago: Moody Publishers, 2014), 1015; and J. A. Motyer, *Isaiah: An Introduction and Commentary*, vol. 20 (Downers Grove, IL: InterVarsity Press, 1999), 67–68.

8. J. Alec Motyer, *Isaiah: An Introduction and Commentary* (Downers Grove, IL: InterVarsity Press, 1999), 66; also, Price "Isaiah 4:2," 812.

9. MercyMe, "All of Creation," 2010.

10. Michael Rydelnik, "Isaiah 7:1–16," *The Moody Handbook of Messianic Prophecy*, 816.

11. Ibid., 817.

12. Motyer, *Isaiah: An Introduction and Commentary*, 88.

13. Rydelnik, "Isaiah 7:1–16," 818–27.

14. Motyer, *Isaiah: An Introduction and Commentary*, 90–91.

15. Rydelnik, "Isaiah 7:1–16," 820.

16. Ibid.

17. Andrew M. Davis, *Exalting Jesus in Isaiah* (Nashville: Holman Reference, 2017), 61–66.

18. Hindson, "Isaiah 9:1–7," 838–39.

19. Warren W. Wiersbe, *Be Comforted: Feeling Secure in the Arms of God* (Colorado Springs: David C. Cook, 2009), 47.

20. Michael Rydelnik and James Spencer, "Isaiah" in *The Moody Bible Commentary*, ed. Michael Rydelnik and Michael Vanlaningham (Chicago: Moody Publishers, 2014), 1024–25.

21. Hindson, "Isaiah 9:1–7," 836.

22. Ibid., 836–37.

23. Wiersbe, *Be Comforted*, 47.

24. John N. Oswalt, *Isaiah: The NIV Application Commentary* (Grand Rapids: Zondervan, 2003), 161.

25. *Merriam-Webster*, s.v. "zeal," https://www.merriam-webster.com/dictionary/zeal.

26. Rydelnik and Spencer, "Isaiah," 1026.

27. Oswalt, *Isaiah*, 189.

WEEK TWO: THE SAVIOR WILL CONQUER SIN AND DEATH

1. Andrew M. Davis, *Exalting Jesus in Isaiah* (Nashville: Holman Reference, 2017), 146.

2. *Merriam-Webster*, s.v. "believe," https://www.merriam-webster.com/dictionary/believe.

3. *Merriam-Webster*, s.v. "hope," https://www.merriam-webster.com/dictionary/hope.

4. Ibid.

5. For example, Psalm 118:22; Isaiah 8:14; Daniel 2:34–35, 44–45; and Zechariah 4:7–10.

6. John N. Oswalt, *Isaiah: The NIV Application Commentary* (Grand Rapids: Zondervan, 2003), 151.

7. Warren W. Wiersbe, *Be Comforted: Feeling Secure in the Arms of God* (Colorado Springs: David C. Cook, 2009), 87.

8. Alfred Martin, *Isaiah*, Everyday Bible Commentary (Chicago: Moody Publishers, 2018), 61–62.

9. Ibid.

10. Michael Gabizon, "Isaiah 30:19–26," *The Moody Handbook of Messianic Prophecy: Studies and Expositions of the Messiah in the Old Testament,* ed. Michael Rydelnik and Edwin Blum (Chicago: Moody Publishers, 2019), 885–93.

11. Ibid., 890.

12. *Merriam-Webster*, s.v. "Shechinah," https://www.merriam-webster.com/dictionary/Shechinah.

13. Gabizon, "Isaiah 30:19–26," 887.

WEEK THREE: THE SAVIOR WITH US

1. Warren W. Wiersbe, *Be Comforted: Feeling Secure in the Arms of God* (Colorado Springs: David C. Cook, 2009), 126.

2. Alfred Martin, *Isaiah*, Everyday Bible Commentary (Chicago: Moody Publishers, 2018), 74.

3. Wiersbe, *Be Comforted,* 126.

4. John N. Oswalt, *Isaiah: The NIV Application Commentary* (Grand Rapids: Zondervan, 2003), 444.

5. James F. Coakley, "Isaiah 35:1–10," *The Moody Handbook of Messianic Prophecy: Studies and Expositions of the Messiah in the Old Testament*, ed. Michael Rydelnik and Edwin Blum (Chicago: Moody Publishers, 2019), 916.

6. Wiersbe, *Be Comforted,* 105.

7. Andrew M. Davis, *Exalting Jesus in Isaiah* (Nashville: Holman Reference, 2017), 229.

8. For ideas on having conversations about Christ and the Christian faith, see *Sent: Living a Life That Invites Others to Jesus* by Heather Holleman and Ashley Holleman (Chicago: Moody Publishers, 2020).

9. Oswalt, *Isaiah*, 468–69.

10. Davis, *Exalting Jesus in Isaiah*, 236.

11. Martin, *Isaiah*, 77.

12. Robert B. Chisholm Jr., "Isaiah 42:1–9," *The Moody Handbook of Messianic Prophecy*, 937.

13. Oswalt, *Isaiah*, 472.

WEEK FOUR: THE SAVIOR'S STRENGTH AND LOVE

1. Andrew M. Davis, *Exalting Jesus in Isaiah* (Nashville: Holman Reference, 2017), 255.

2. I tell more about this experience in *His Last Words: What Jesus Taught and Prayed in His Final Hours* and in *Surviving Sorrow: A Mother's Guide to Living with Loss*.

3. John N. Oswalt, *Isaiah: The NIV Application Commentary* (Grand Rapids: Zondervan, 2003), 485.

4. Warren W. Wiersbe, *Be Comforted: Feeling Secure in the Arms of God* (Colorado Springs: David C. Cook, 2009), 147.

5. Davis, *Exalting Jesus in Isaiah*, 306.

6. Ibid., 309.

WEEK FIVE: THE SAVIOR'S SACRIFICE

1. Warren W. Wiersbe, *Be Comforted: Feeling Secure in the Arms of God* (Colorado Springs: David C. Cook, 2009), 155.

2. Elliott E. Johnson, "Isaiah 50:4–11," *The Moody Handbook of Messianic Prophecy: Studies and Expositions of the Messiah in the Old Testament*, ed. Michael Rydelnik and Edwin Blum (Chicago: Moody Publishers, 2019), 961–64.

3. The Israel Museum, Jerusalem, "The Dead Sea Scrolls," https://www.imj.org.il/en/wings/shrine-book/dead-sea-scrolls. "The most outstanding of the Dead Sea Scrolls is undoubtedly the Isaiah Scroll (Manuscript A)—the only biblical scroll from Qumran that has been preserved in its entirety (it is 734 cm long). This scroll is also one of the oldest to have been preserved; scholars estimate that it was written around 100 BCE. In addition, among the scrolls are some twenty additional copies of Isaiah, as well as six pesharim (sectarian exegetical works) based on the book; Isaiah is also frequently quoted in other scrolls. The prominence of this particular book is consistent with the Community's messianic beliefs, since Isaiah (Judean Kingdom, 8th century BCE) is known for his prophecies concerning the End of Days."

4. David Limbaugh, *Finding Jesus in The Old Testament* (Washington, DC: Regnery Publishing, 2017), 288.

5. Andrew M. Davis, *Exalting Jesus in Isaiah* (Nashville: Holman Reference, 2017), 318.

6. Wiersbe, *Be Comforted*, 162.

7. F. B. Meyer, *Christ in Isaiah: Expositions of Isaiah XL–LV* (New York: Revell 1895), 158.

8. Wiersbe, *Be Comforted*, 162.

9. Michael Rydelnik and James Spencer, "Isaiah," in *The Moody Bible Commentary*, ed. Michael Rydelnik and Michael Vanlaningham (Chicago: Moody Publishers, 2014), 1089–90.

10. Alfred Martin, *Isaiah*, Everyday Bible Commentary (Chicago: Moody Publishers, 2018), 109.

11. Rydelnik and Spencer, "Isaiah," 1091.

WEEK SIX: THE SAVIOR'S EVERLASTING PEACE

1. Andrew M. Davis, *Exalting Jesus in Isaiah* (Nashville: Holman Reference, 2017), 335.

2. Michael Rydelnik and James Spencer, "Isaiah," *The Moody Bible Commentary*, ed. Michael Rydelnik and Michael Vanlaningham (Chicago: Moody Publishers, 2014), 1097.

3. Edward E. Hindson, "Isaiah 61:1–6," *The Moody Handbook of Messianic Prophecy: Studies and Expositions of the Messiah in the Old Testament*, ed. Michael Rydelnik and Edwin Blum (Chicago: Moody Publishers, 2019), 986.

4. Ibid., 991.

Advice from one grieving mom to others

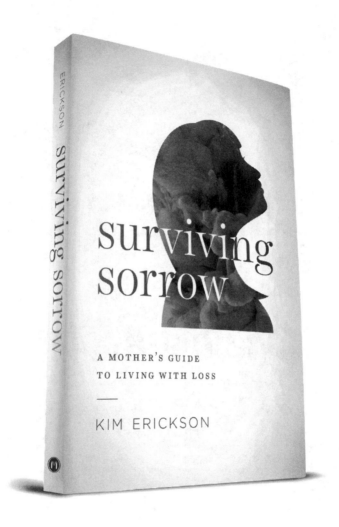